PAUL RICOEUR

Paul Ricoeur is one of the most important critical thinkers to emerge in the twentieth century. His unique 'theory of reading' or *hermeneutics* extends far beyond the reading of literary works to build into a theory for the reading of 'life'. As a result of this, such works as *Philosophy of the Will, The Rule of Metaphor, Time and Narrative* and *Oneself as Another* have impacted upon the widest range of disciplines, from literary criticism and philosophy to history, religion, legal studies and politics.

In this stimulating guide, Karl Simms explores Ricoeur's most influential ideas, touching upon such concepts as good and evil, psychoanalysis, hermeneutics, metaphor, narrative, ethics, politics and justice. Crucially, he also places these ideas in context and looks at their continuing impact, in this way introducing important trends in contemporary thought. Throughout this volume, the author prepares us for our own reading of Ricoeur's work, and this culminates in an extensively annotated guide to his major publications.

Refreshingly clear and impressively comprehensive, *Paul Ricoeur* is the essential guide to an essential theorist.

Karl Simms is Director of the English-Philosophy joint programme at the University of Liverpool and a lecturer in English Language and Literature. He is the editor of *Ethics and the Subject* (1997), *Language and the Subject* (1997) and *Translating Sensitive Texts* (1997).

ROUTLEDGE CRITICAL THINKERS
essential guides for literary studies

Series Editor: Robert Eaglestone, Royal Holloway, University of London

Routledge Critical Thinkers is a series of accessible introductions to key figures in contemporary critical thought.

With a unique focus on historical and intellectual contexts, each volume examines a key theorist's:

- significance
- motivation
- key ideas and their sources
- impact on other thinkers

Concluding with extensively annotated guides to further reading, *Routledge Critical Thinkers* are the literature student's passport to today's most exciting critical thought.

Already available:
Jean Baudrillard by Richard J. Lane
Maurice Blanchot by Ullrich Haase and William Large
Judith Butler by Sara Salih
Gilles Deleuze by Claire Colebrook
Sigmund Freud by Pamela Thurschwell
Martin Heidegger by Timothy Clark
Fredric Jameson by Adam Roberts
Jean-François Lyotard by Simon Malpas
Paul de Man by Martin McQuillan
Paul Ricoeur by Karl Simms
Edward Said by Bill Ashcroft and Pal Ahluwalia
Gayatri Chakravorty Spivak by Stephen Morton

For further details on this series, see www.literature.routledge.com/rct

PAUL RICOEUR

Karl Simms

Routledge
Taylor & Francis Group

LONDON AND NEW YORK

First published 2003
by Routledge
11 New Fetter Lane, London EC4P 4EE

Simultaneously published in the USA and Canada
by Routledge
29 West 35th Street, New York, NY 10001

Routledge is an imprint of the Taylor & Francis Group

© 2003 Karl Simms

Typeset in Perpetua by
Florence Production Ltd, Stoodleigh, Devon
Printed and bound in Great Britain by
TJ International Ltd, Padstow, Cornwall

British Library Cataloguing in Publication Data
A catalogue record for this book is available from the British Library.

Library of Congress Cataloging in Publication Data
Simms, Karl.
  Paul Ricoeur/Karl Simms.
    p. cm. – (Routledge critical thinkers)
  Includes bibliographical references and index.
  1. Ricoeur, Paul.   I. Title.   II. Series.
  B2430.R554.S56 2003
  194 – dc21   2002068223

ISBN 0–415–23636–3 (hbk)
ISBN 0–415–23637–1 (pbk)

TO MY WIFE TRACY,
WITH LOVE

CONTENTS

SERIES EDITOR'S PREFACE

The books in this series offer introductions to major critical thinkers who have influenced literary studies and the humanities. The *Routledge Critical Thinkers* series provides the books you can turn to first when a new name or concept appears in your studies.

Each book will equip you to approach a key thinker's original texts by explaining her or his key ideas, putting them into context and, perhaps most importantly, showing you why this thinker is considered to be significant. The emphasis is on concise, clearly written guides which do not presuppose a specialist knowledge. Although the focus is on particular figures, the series stresses that no critical thinker ever existed in a vacuum but, instead, emerged from a broader intellectual, cultural and social history. Finally, these books will act as a bridge between you and the thinker's original texts: not replacing them but rather complementing what she or he wrote.

These books are necessary for a number of reasons. In his 1997 autobiography, *Not Entitled*, the literary critic Frank Kermode wrote of a time in the 1960s:

> On beautiful summer lawns, young people lay together all night, recovering from their daytime exertions and listening to a troupe of Balinese musicians. Under their blankets or their sleeping bags, they would chat drowsily about the gurus of the time ... What they repeated was largely hearsay; hence my

> lunchtime suggestion, quite impromptu, for a series of short, very cheap books
> offering authoritative but intelligible introductions to such figures.

There is still a need for 'authoritative and intelligible introductions'. But this series reflects a different world from the 1960s. New thinkers have emerged and the reputations of others have risen and fallen, as new research has developed. New methodologies and challenging ideas have spread through arts and humanities. The study of literature is no longer – if it ever was – simply the study and evaluation of poems, novels and plays. It is also the study of ideas, issues, and difficulties which arise in any literary text and in its interpretation. Other arts and humanities subjects have changed in analogous ways.

With these changes, new problems have emerged. The ideas and issues behind these radical changes in the humanities are often presented without reference to wider contexts or as theories which you can simply 'add on' to the texts you read. Certainly, there's nothing wrong with picking out selected ideas or using what comes to hand – indeed, some thinkers have argued that this is, in fact, all we can do. However, it is sometimes forgotten that each new idea comes from the pattern and development of somebody's thought and it is important to study the range and context of their ideas. Against theories 'floating in space', the *Routledge Critical Thinkers* series places key thinkers and their ideas firmly back in their contexts.

More than this, these books reflect the need to go back to the thinker's own texts and ideas. Every interpretation of an idea, even the most seemingly innocent one, offers its own 'spin', implicitly or explicitly. To read only books on a thinker, rather than texts by that thinker, is to deny yourself a chance of making up your own mind. Sometimes what makes a significant figure's work hard to approach is not so much its style or content as the feeling of not knowing where to start. The purpose of these books is to give you a 'way in' by offering an accessible overview of these thinkers' ideas and works and by guiding your further reading, starting with each thinker's own texts. To use a metaphor from the philosopher Ludwig Wittgenstein (1889–1951), these books are ladders, to be thrown away after you have climbed to the next level. Not only, then, do they equip you to approach new ideas, but also they empower you, by leading you back to the theorist's own texts and encouraging you to develop your own informed opinions.

Finally, these books are necessary because, just as intellectual needs have changed, the education systems around the world – the contexts in which introductory books are usually read – have changed radically, too. What was suitable for the minority higher education system of the 1960s is not suitable for the larger, wider, more diverse, high technology education systems of the twenty-first century. These changes call not just for new, up-to-date, introductions but new methods of presentation. The presentational aspects of *Routledge Critical Thinkers* have been developed with today's students in mind.

Each book in the series has a similar structure. They begin with a section offering an overview of the life and ideas of each thinker and explain why she or he is important. The central section of each book discusses the thinker's key ideas, their context, evolution and reception. Each book concludes with a survey of the thinker's impact, outlining how their ideas have been taken up and developed by others. In addition, there is a detailed final section suggesting and describing books for further reading. This is not a 'tacked-on' section but an integral part of each volume. In the first part of this section you will find brief descriptions of the thinker's key works: following this, information on the most useful critical works and, in some cases, on relevant websites. This section will guide you in your reading, enabling you to follow your interests and develop your own projects. Throughout each book, references are given in what is known as the Harvard system (the author and the date of a work cited are given in the text and you can look up the full details in the bibliography at the back). This offers a lot of information in very little space. The books also explain technical terms and use boxes to describe events or ideas in more detail, away from the main emphasis of the discussion. Boxes are also used at times to highlight definitions of terms frequently used or coined by a thinker. In this way, the boxes serve as a kind of glossary, easily identified when flicking through the book.

The thinkers in the series are 'critical' for three reasons. First, they are examined in the light of subjects which involve criticism: principally literary studies or English and cultural studies, but also other disciplines which rely on the criticism of books, ideas, theories and unquestioned assumptions. Second, they are critical because studying their work will provide you with a 'tool kit' for your own informed critical reading and thought, which will make you critical. Third, these thinkers are critical because they are crucially important: they deal with ideas and questions which can overturn conventional understandings of the world, of texts, of everything we take for granted, leaving us with a deeper understanding of what we already knew and with new ideas.

No introduction can tell you everything. However, by offering a way into critical thinking, this series hopes to begin to engage you in an activity which is productive, constructive and potentially life-changing.

WHY RICOEUR?

Paul Ricoeur is probably the most wide-ranging of thinkers alive in the world today. Although nominally a philosopher, his work has also cut across the subjects of religion and biblical exegesis, history, literary criticism, psychoanalysis, legal studies and politics, as well as having implications for sociology, psychology and linguistics. And yet despite this disparity of subject matter, there is an underlying continuity to his thought. His writings are always informed by an underlying intention that they should be *good* works, which means not only that they should be of high quality (notwithstanding the sheer quantity of his output, Ricoeur's work is always meticulously researched and referenced), but also that they should be ethically good. Whatever the subject matter he turns to, Ricoeur always defends the values of religious belief and social justice. For these reasons he is arguably the world's most respected living philosopher, but he is not the trendiest. Written in a sober and patient (some would say verbose) style, Ricoeur's works seek in academic discourse what he hopes for in society – co-operation. Consequently, he is lacking in the iconoclasm of other French thinkers such as Jacques Derrida or Jean Baudrillard, and instead is constantly trying to build bridges between philosophical traditions. Rather than loudly proclaim a difference between his thought and that of others, he quietly draws out its similarities. This is a self-effacing way of proceeding, which can give the impression that Ricoeur is derivative of those he reads. But closer examination reveals him to be an original thinker, whose originality lies in building on the thought of others, always adding something more, rather than adopting an oppositional stance.

Ricoeur is a philosopher of faith rather than a philosopher of suspicion. This does not only mean that he has faith in the religious sense. It also means that, as a consequence of his religious faith, he also has faith in metaphysics, or the tradition of thinking. More particularly, he has faith in the language or discourse in which thinking is expressed. He sees it as his mission to draw out the hidden intentions behind written works, not to expose works as deceptive. Written works are like the Delphic oracle: they may hide their meaning from us, but they do not lie. This faith in human discourse is expressed through Ricoeur's theory of reading, *hermeneutics*, which is explained in Chapter 2. The premise behind hermeneutics is that written works are the route to understanding the meaning of life. This in turn presupposes that life *has* meaning, but this is a virtuous circle for Ricoeur (he calls it the 'hermeneutic circle'): written works have meaning because they are reflective of life, and life gains meaning through its ability to be represented in written works. Ricoeur's philosophy is simultaneously a philosophy of life and a philosophy of reading. It is this which enables it to be universally applicable: whatever discipline we are in, be it history, psychoanalysis, literary criticism or whatever, that discipline is constructed through texts, and those texts each in different ways conceal their true meaning that hermeneutics reveals – the meaning of life. By extension, life itself can be 'read', or interpreted, and that interpretation itself reveals life to be a narrative. Our ethical aim is, according to Ricoeur, to make the story of our life a good story.

RICOEUR'S CAREER

Paul Ricoeur was born at Valence, south of Lyons, in France, 1913 (Regan 1996: 4). He first became interested in philosophy in his final year of high school, 1929–30 (Ricoeur 1995a: 3). He then spent two years (1931–3) at the unfashionable provincial University of Rennes, studying for the entrance examination to the prestigious École Normale Supérieure in Paris. He was a brilliant student of Latin and Greek, but failed the philosophy section of the entrance examination. Hence he remained at Rennes for a further year, and took an MA in philosophy;

his dissertation was on 'The Problem of God'. At this time Ricoeur developed the interest which has informed his work to the present day, that of the relationship 'between philosophy and biblical faith' (Ricoeur 1995a: 6).

In 1934–5 Ricoeur spent a year at the Sorbonne, where he met his intellectual hero, the Christian philosopher Gabriel Marcel (1889–1973), celebrated for having coined the term 'existentialism'. In 1935 Ricoeur came second out of three hundred candidates in the *agré-gation*, an examination entitling the best students in any particular year to teach, and consequently he was appointed to a number of provincial teaching posts from 1935 to 1940. It was at this time that Ricoeur first became known as an author, publishing articles on Christian socialism and pacifism.

In 1940 (during the Second World War) Ricoeur was called up for military service, and, despite his pacifism, was awarded a medal for bravery. He was soon captured, however, and spent five years in a prisoner of war camp in eastern Germany. There he helped set up an unofficial 'University of the Prison Camp', where a group of prisoners would lecture to one another and collaborate in research. It was difficult to get hold of books other than German ones, and thus it was that Ricoeur read the work of the German philosopher Edmund Husserl (1859–1938) for the first time, and translated Husserl's most famous book, *Ideas* (1913), into French. Despite conditions of dreadful hardship (which included there being scarcely any paper available), Ricoeur also began a book on the German Christian existentialist philosopher Karl Jaspers (1883–1959), co-written with a fellow prisoner, Mikel Dufrenne, and a comparative study of Jaspers and Marcel. Husserl, Jaspers and Marcel were to be the three major influences on Ricoeur's writing throughout the 1950s.

In 1950 Ricoeur was awarded his PhD on the basis of his translation of Husserl, and in recognition of the first part of Ricoeur's own *Philosophy of the Will*, *The Voluntary and the Involuntary*. Ricoeur taught at Le Chambon, 1945–8, and Strasbourg, 1948–55. In 1956 he was appointed Chair of General Philosophy at the Sorbonne. In 1960 the second part of his *Philosophy of the Will* was published, itself in two parts, *Fallible Man* and *The Symbolism of Evil*. It was at this point that Ricoeur became the best known philosopher in France, and a figure of international standing: as his biographer writes, 'his classes at the Sorbonne were jammed and loudspeakers had to be set up in the courtyard so the overflow crowd could hear him. Hundreds of students asked him to direct their theses' (Reagan 1996: 24). His success was consolidated by the publication of his next book, *Freud and Philosophy*, in 1965.

Meanwhile, Ricoeur had written several articles criticising the French university system, and in 1967 he left the Sorbonne to become the Dean of the Faculty of Letters at the new 'experimental' University of Nanterre, just outside Paris. (Nanterre was France's first purpose-built campus university, and as such was designed to emulate the residential universities and colleges of the US and UK.) By 1969, however, the student body at Nanterre had become dominated by extreme left-wing groups, who staged a series of demonstrations and occupations on the campus, protesting against various 'bourgeois' aspects of French society, the education system and the Nanterre administration. Eventually, Ricoeur was forced to call in the police to 'banalise' the campus, and restore control of it to the authorities. This culminated in a full-scale riot involving several hundred police and students, and causing several million francs worth of damage. Although he had been blameless, this harmed both Ricoeur's reputation and his relations with the French government, and so in 1970 he resigned, and embarked on a self-imposed exile in Belgium (Louvain), the US (Chicago) and Canada (Toronto), returning to Nanterre in 1973 and then only for a few months each year.

During the 1970s Ricoeur published *The Rule of Metaphor* (1975) and several articles which were later to be collected in *Hermeneutics and the Human Sciences* (1981) and *From Text to Action* (1986); at this time it was more likely for Ricoeur's work to be published in English translation than in French, and as his fame grew abroad, so it diminished in his home country. In 1980, aged 67, he retired from Nanterre; it is a mark of Ricoeur's extraordinary longevity that many of the works for which he is best known have been written since that date.

During the early 1980s Ricoeur published his three-volume *Time and Narrative*, which led to his rehabilitation in France, to be succeeded by one of his most important books, *Oneself as Another* (1990). Ricoeur finally retired his post at the University of Chicago in 1991; in the same year he was awarded the prize in philosophy from the French Academy. Subsequently, Ricoeur has continued to lecture, and to write exten-sively in political philosophy and theories of justice, including the short book *The Just* (1995).

THIS BOOK

The 'Key Ideas' section of this book presents Ricoeur's ideas in roughly the order in which he developed them. As we saw above, the idea for which Ricoeur is perhaps best known is 'hermeneutics', or interpretation theory. His influence on literary theory and criticism is consequently direct, rather than being mediated by the works of disciples, as has been the case with other French philosophers and theorists of Ricoeur's generation. Moreover, Ricoeur is one of the few philosophers (as opposed to literary critics and theorists) to have consistently taken literature, or literary language, as his object of study. His *Time and Narrative*, as well as contributing to a theory of the relationship between narrative and life, is also a series of exercises in the criticism of specific narrative texts, and as such is exemplary of how the hermeneutic model of literary criticism can be put into practice. His *The Rule of Metaphor*, as well as contributing to the theory of metaphor in and of itself, abounds in literary examples, and anticipates *Time and Narrative* in its realisation that, since our understanding of the world is articulated through metaphor, and since metaphor is essentially a literary phenomenon, literature has a fundamental quality of instructing us in how life is lived by humans. And even a relatively early work, *The Symbolism of Evil*, in taking myths as its primary theme, is essentially textual in its concerns, and again not only provides a *theory* of the symbol, but also *shows* how symbols lend themselves to interpretation in the practice of reading texts.

Ricoeur is what he would call an 'epigenetic' thinker, which means that his thought is accumulative. Throughout a very long career from the 1940s to the present day, there is a continuity behind his work; thus, each of his ideas is a development, rather than a negation, of his previous. Hence each chapter that follows refers not only to Ricoeur's thinking at a particular time, but also to the continuity of that thought with his previous ideas. You may wish to begin reading at any chapter that you will find helpful in explaining a particular area of Ricoeur's thinking that you have encountered, or you may wish to read the chapters in sequence, to gain a sense of the progressive accumulation of his ideas. In either case, the aim of this book is not to give an exhaustive account of Ricoeur's ideas, but to provide a way in to reading Ricoeur's own texts. Consequently, the 'Further Reading' section at the end of the book begins by giving information on Ricoeur's own works; some secondary texts are also included, but with an eye to their usefulness in aiding the reading of the primary texts.

KEY IDEAS

1

GOOD AND EVIL

In the 1950s Ricoeur had the ambitious aim of completing a monumental three-part *Philosophy of the Will*. In the event, only the first two parts, *The Voluntary and the Involuntary* and *Finitude and Guilt*, were completed (although the latter was itself subdivided into two parts, *Fallible Man* and *The Symbolism of Evil*). These early works form an important precursor to Ricoeur's 'hermeneutic' philosophy, which is described in Chapters 2–7 that follow: whatever area of philosophy Ricoeur subsequently turns his attention to, he is always consistent with the ideals he was to set himself in *Philosophy of the Will*.

Ricoeur's early thought conceives of life as a 'dialectic': on the one hand, I am master of myself and choose and will courses of action (this is the 'voluntary'), while on the other hand I am subjected to the necessity of being in the world, with all the things beyond my control which that implies, along with the necessity of my being who I am – I have a certain character along with an unconscious mind that defies my will (this being the 'involuntary'). How we negotiate our lives between the freedom accorded us as human beings and the constraints that are imposed upon us by the fact of our being humans living in the world is, then, the departure point for Ricoeur's philosophy. Moreover, as an overtly Christian philosopher, Ricoeur is interested in the way good and evil are replicated in, or at least show themselves in, the human dialectic between free will and necessity.

THE VOLUNTARY AND THE INVOLUNTARY: WILL AND THE PASSIONS

Ricoeur's philosophy is motivated by a Christian need to explain the origins of evil in the world, and thus to answer the questions that this problem carries with it, such as *Why* is there evil in the world?, and *Why* do people commit evil deeds? His starting point in answering these questions is to investigate one of the ways in which the dialectic of life shows itself, in the conflict between the will and the 'passions' – our wants and needs prompted by such biological factors as hunger, sex drive, etc. In order to conduct his investigation, Ricoeur adopts the *phenomenological* method of the German philosopher Edmund Husserl (1859–1938). However, while adopting Husserl's methods, Ricoeur goes some way beyond his conclusions.

For Ricoeur, Husserl does not really *understand* the passions (the involuntary), because he does not grasp that there is a *reciprocal* relation between mind and body – Husserl *describes* through the mind alone. Ricoeur, meanwhile, draws a distinction between *description* and *understanding*: passing beyond description to understanding consists in acknowledging the *relation* between mind and body, voluntary and involuntary. However, since there is only one will (the voluntary), but there are many (involuntary) passions, a *description of the will* is still the starting point for Ricoeur's attempt to 'synthesise' the voluntary will with the involuntary passions, because explanation consists in proceeding from the simple to the complex.

Ricoeur's (1966: 6) description reveals, first, that to will is a type of act, seen as a triad: 'To say "I will" means first "I decide", second "I move my body", third "I consent"'. Ricoeur follows Husserl's rule that 'all consciousness is consciousness of something', and by analogy claims that all willing must have an action as its object – all willing is willing to act. There are three 'modes', or ways, of willing: *decision*, *movement* and *consent*. When I *decide*, the object of my willing is 'a project I form . . . to be done by me in accord with my abilities' (Ricoeur 1966: 7). When I *move my body*, an action is carried out. When I *consent*, I acquiesce to necessity: the necessity that things are as they are, that I am alive in a biological body which has its limitations.

According to Ricoeur, each of these three dimensions of willing also involves the will's opposite, the involuntary. First, when I make a *decision*, it 'stands in an original relation not only to the project which is its

PHENOMENOLOGY

Phenomenology is the philosophy developed by Husserl, most notably in his book *Ideas* (1913), and in his series of lectures published as *Cartesian Meditations* (1931). Phenomenology starts from the position that whatever I perceive I perceive through the senses. Husserl *suspends his judgement* as to whether what his senses tell him is true: the phenomenologist is engaged in a mental exercise, or thought experiment, whereby judgements *about* the world around him are 'bracketed off'. This allows him to engage in phenomenological, or *eidetic* (*eidos* is Greek for 'form'), analysis, which reveals things as they appear as phenomena, this allegedly being more 'essential' than as they 'really' are, how things really are being a matter of mere speculation. So, a phenomenological analysis of a tree, for example, would not focus on those aspects of the tree that could be reduced to scientific description, such as its chemical composition, its dimensions etc., but rather would concentrate on how the tree appears *to me*: its movement in the breeze, its changing shape according to the angle from which it is viewed, its changing colour according to the time of day and time of year, etc. None of these aspects of the tree is solely dependent on what the tree consists of as a material object; rather, each is dependent on how the tree, myself, and the world around myself and the tree, all interact with one another. This description of the tree is not a description of how the tree is perceived, although that is its starting point. Rather, it is a description of the phenomenologist's *consciousness* of the tree. Perhaps a more important thing than trees that can be described or analysed phenomenologically is consciousness itself. This allows the phenomenologist to enter a happy state of *apperception* (perceiving that he is perceiving): in this state, the phenomenologist's consciousness is interacting with itself; he is in a state of *self-consciousness*. This, for Husserl, is the *only* way to examine consciousness: consciousness is always consciousness *of* something, even if that something is consciousness itself.

specific object, but also the motives which justify it' (Ricoeur 1966: 7). In other words, I do not just do things for no reason. The reasons I have in making a decision are a form of the involuntary – Ricoeur calls them 'motivation'. Second, in *moving my body*, I must recognise that my body is as much governed by involuntary motions as by willing: this does not just mean things like breathing, but also when I do things by habit – my *will* to do those things is being in some sense cheated on those occasions. And third, when I *consent*, I give myself over to something other than me over which I have no control, and that something is a form of necessity. There are thus three modes of the involuntary standing in relation to the three modes of the voluntary act: the decision is tempered by motivation, the movement of the body is tempered by involuntary motion, and consent is tempered by necessity. These relations then become the lever for Ricoeur to 'reconquer' the Cartesian *cogito*.

In Descartes (and the same is true of Husserl), the *cogito* is something to be performed – it is a mental act. Its performance leads to a separation of the soul (or thinking) from the body, so that the body is then viewed so to speak from the outside, that is, from the perspective of pure thought. But for Ricoeur, because the *cogito* is a mental act, it is an act of the will. As such, it contains within it the relationship with willing's other (motivation, motion and necessity) as described in his analysis of the will. In this way, Ricoeur 'extends' the *cogito* to include what Descartes and Husserl excluded from it, namely the personal body. Descartes, says Ricoeur, abstracts *acts* into *facts*. Ricoeur's criticism of Descartes, and of his follower Husserl, is that they are philosophers of the Ego: '*Ego* cogito, ergo sum'; '*I* think therefore

THE CARTESIAN *COGITO*

The proposition 'I think therefore I am' is commonly referred to as the 'Cartesian *cogito*', after its inventor, the French philosopher and mathematician René Descartes (1596–1650), and its Latin formulation, *cogito ergo sum*. Descartes arrived at the *cogito* through his Method. The Method, which was an entirely novel departure in philosophy in Descartes' day, consists in starting without any presuppositions, and looking at the world around you from the standpoint of not expecting to find anything in particular. In looking around, you then adopt a *sceptical* attitude, questioning whatever you perceive. Doing this, Descartes discovered that he can doubt that the world around him is the real world (a malicious demon inside his head might be deceiving him, or he might be dreaming), or he can even doubt that the world exists at all. However, the one thing Descartes cannot doubt is that he is thinking. From this he deduces that he must exist, must be an existing being in order to do the thinking he's engaged in – hence, 'I think therefore I am'.

I am'. This leads to an arid, sterile circularity. The Cartesian knows that he is thinking because he is thinking, which is all well and good, but what does he *do*? The phenomenologist, meanwhile, suspends his judgement, rather than doubts that the world exists, but is still caught up in his mental exercise of apperception, leaving the world unchanged. As a Christian (and a socialist) Ricoeur wants to change the world, but for a philosophy to change the world it must intersect with the world in some way. Ricoeur's acknowledgement of the will's being tempered by necessity, which is really an acknowledgement of the influence of the body on any mental act (including the act of performing the *cogito*), is a way of bringing the reality of the outside world into the mental world of the Cartesian and the phenomenologist. As Ricoeur (1966: 14) puts it, 'the Ego must more radically renounce the covert claim of all consciousness, must abandon its wish to posit itself, so that it can receive the nourishing and inspiring spontaneity which breaks the sterile circle of the self's constant return to itself'.

According to Ricoeur, breaking the circle of the self's constant return to itself is a way of passing 'from objectivity to existence'. The Cartesian sees the person as divided into the body, which as an object has *objective* existence, and a soul, which has *subjective* existence. In removing the distinction between soul and body – or, more precisely, in demonstrating that a soul is impossible, so long as we are in the world, without a body – Ricoeur unites the objective with the subjective under the single heading of 'existence'. Existence is what subjects have who have the capacity for acknowledging that they have bodies in the material world. Achieving this state of existence, says Ricoeur (1966: 14), 'requires that I participate actively in *my incarnation as a mystery*'. To 'participate actively in my incarnation' means on the one hand to think of myself through the thought of my having a body, and on the other hand to decide, to move and to consent, all of which in some sense involve my body controlling me, to however small a degree.

But why 'as a mystery'? 'What to do with the body' has always been a problem for philosophers in the Cartesian tradition, such as Husserl. Ricoeur wants to claim that my having a body is not a philosophical *problem*, but a *mystery*. The distinction is one originally made by the French Christian philosopher Gabriel Marcel (1889–1973): a problem is something to be solved, but a mystery is something which, although we do not know the answer to it, does not require an answer, does not need solving. That I have a body as a pre-given is what remains mysterious (as opposed to problematic) for me. According to Ricoeur, this mystery is a condition of being able to posit the *cogito* in the first place. The *cogito* is an act of positing myself, but in order to do this I must participate in the condition that makes the *cogito* possible in the first place, namely my having a body. Ricoeur's (1966: 18) aim is to restore 'the original concord of vague consciousness with its body and its world'. The mystery is to be understood as a reconciliation between Cartesian consciousness (self-consciousness) and objectivity.

Ricoeur's philosophy, however, is not only a 'philosophy of mystery', but also a 'philosophy of paradox'. The 'paradox' is that without the necessity of my having a body and being in the world, I could not have free will, but that free will is tempered by those necessities. Ricoeur identifies three modes of freedom, corresponding to the three modes of the will: freedom of choice, freedom of movement and freedom of consent. Each of these freedoms is 'paradoxical' in the sense of requiring some sort of negotiation between one way of thinking and its opposite.

Freedom of choice is tempered by need, but need can be rejected as the motive for an action. This leads to an experience of sacrifice: for example, 'man is capable of choosing between his hunger *and* something else' (Ricoeur 1966: 93). Similarly, without chastity sexuality would not be *human* sexuality. Needs, then, are another example of the 'dialectic' of human life. ('Dialectical' here means having something by rejecting its opposite, a definition which Ricoeur again borrows from Gabriel Marcel.) I have a *human* need for food because I can will to sacrifice it; I have a *human* need for sex because I have the will to sacrifice it, etc.

Something analogous is true of freedom of movement, which is tempered by emotion and habit, and freedom of consent, which in the very words 'freedom of consent' is revealed the paradoxical nature of this formula: consenting is the voluntary act of surrendering freedom. All of these paradoxical formulations describe modes of specifically *human* freedom, and human freedom is limited by the negative concepts – need, emotion or habit and necessity – which determine it by the possibility of the will's rejecting them: they are what Ricoeur calls 'limit concepts' (a notion borrowed from the German Christian existentialist Karl Jaspers (1883–1969)). 'These limit concepts', says Ricoeur (1966: 486), 'have no other function here than to help us understand, by contrast, the condition of a will which is reciprocal with an involuntary'.

EXISTENTIALISM

A philosophy initially developed by Gabriel Marcel and Karl Jaspers in the 1920s, and which takes *existence* to be that which must be *assumed* by any thinking being. Consequently, existentialism is opposed to Cartesianism, which sets out to prove existence from the fact of thinking. Existentialists take existence, not thinking, to be primary, but the fact of existence is not something that can be *proved*: rather, existence is a *pre-given*. Marcel and Jaspers were Christians, and took existence to be a gift from God, who Himself does not *exist*, since existence is something that only a being in the world can experience, whereas God is outside the world, eternal. Humans are the only animals who can *experience* existence, rather than merely exist as such, and it is their task in life to interpret that experience.

After the Second World War the French philosopher Jean-Paul Sartre (1905–80) imported the *materialist* theory of Karl Marx – that physical reality is the only reality – into existentialism, and thereby took existentialism in an atheist direction, causing Marcel to repudiate the term 'existentialist'. For Sartre, as for his Algerian contemporary Albert Camus (1913–60), the alternative is not between existence and eternity, but between existence and nothing. Existence is the choice or decision not to commit suicide, although again humans are the only animals capable of making this choice. Moreover, humans define themselves not through their thoughts, but through their actions: 'to be is to do'. Insofar as Ricoeur is influenced by existentialism, he agrees with Sartre concerning the importance of action, but is much closer to Marcel and Jaspers in preserving the at least equal importance of interpretation of that action as a defining characteristic of human life.

FALLIBLE MAN: THE FAULT, DISPROPORTION AND FRAGILITY

If man can only be understood as existent, which is to say, as a negoti-ation between a thinking, willing being who acts, and a being in the world who is subjected to the necessities that the world, including his own body, imposes on him, then this 'paradoxical' existence seems a long way from the certainty that Descartes found in his thinking. In fact, the 'paradoxical' nature of man's existence makes it look quite a fragile affair. There is a fault running through man's existence, like a fault-line in the geological sense. In geology, a fault lies between two different strata of rock (by analogy, the willing soul and the involuntary passions), which when rubbed together produce disharmonious effects. This fracturing, in man as in geology, is a weakness; in man it is the weakness that is inherent in the constitution of man himself: without it, man would not be man. It is the weakness of being comprised of soul and body as a totality. The fallible nature of this existence is, for Ricoeur (1965a: 203), what allows the possibility of moral evil: 'the *possibility* of moral evil is inherent in man's constitution'. Fallibility is the possibility of fault, of disrupture between the soul and the passions, which really means the possibility of succumbing to the temptations which the passions present. There are two points to note here. First, Ricoeur is not claiming that man is inherently evil – merely that he contains within him an inherent *possibility* of evil. Second, evil is not an external, metaphysical force that is presented to man as an object – it is not, for example, Satan, if 'Satan' means a kind of other person who brings evil into the world. Evil is a possibility which man is born with – whether he realises this possibility or not is up to him.

If we hold Ricoeur's first 'working hypothesis' in *Fallible Man*, that 'the possibility of evil appears inscribed in the innermost structure of human reality', then it becomes necessary to hold his second hypothesis, that man is not identical with himself: for example, in the disjunction between his will and the necessity of his being as analysed in *The Voluntary and the Involuntary*. *Fallible Man* then becomes an analysis of the ways in which this 'disproportion' between man and himself may be measured. 'This "disproportion" of self to self', says Ricoeur (1965a: 4) 'would be the *ratio* of fallibility', by which he means two things: first, that the disproportion between self and self is the *reason* behind man's fallibility, and second, that man is fallible *according to the amount* of non-coincidence with himself. The core of *Fallible Man* is a discussion of the three ways in which the disproportion of man's self to himself may be measured. These three ways are in *imagination*, which comes from man's reflecting upon himself; in *character*, which comes from the practicality of living in the world; and in *feeling*, which comes from man's having emotions. Each of these three types of disproportion are, for Ricoeur, moments of *fragility*, whereby man is prone to err: hence imagination, character and feeling (or my mind, my self and my heart) are each fragile.

IMAGINATION

Ricoeur's analysis of imagination starts from a position of what he calls a *pathétique of misery*. '*Pathétique*' is to be understood in the Greek sense of *pathos*, the sadness which comes out of a tragic situation. The *pathétique* of misery is 'pre-comprehended', which is to say, it is a condition of man's being before all thought or consciousness, or before the alleged self-consciousness of the *cogito*. Why is man born into a *pathétique* of misery? Because he is finite. This means not only that he only lives for a limited amount of time, but also that the time he experiences in consciousness is less than his total time on earth: 'my birth is an event for others, not for myself', says Ricoeur (1965a: 36). My life is comprised, if I am conscious, of a series of 'heres': 'I am here now', I might say, and then remember this instance of the 'here' in the future. But 'my place of birth does not appear among the "heres" of my life and cannot therefore be their source' (Ricoeur 1965a: 37). So, in order to comprehend my life as a whole, I must adopt a *perspective* or *point of view*: I view my birth not from a past perception of a 'here', but by in some sense stepping outside myself, and seeing myself as others would see me. In doing this I am already going some way towards 'transgressing' the finitude of my life, and I perform a similar transgression in order to realise that my life *is* finite, and then to discourse upon that finitude. This is the first moment of man's fragility.

CHARACTER

My being born is an *event* for others, but merely a *fact* for me. Contemplating this 'draws my attention to my state of being already born'; moreover, 'my birth is the already-thereness of my character' (Ricoeur 1965a: 96), which brings us to the second moment of man's fragility. *Character* is constant; however I might change, and whatever points of view I might adopt, I shall always have the same character. This is so by definition: if I were to change all of my opinions and all of my ways of behaving, it is true that I would no longer have the same character, but then I would no longer be the same person. But even that radical change on my part would require a decision which would come out of . . . well, my character, of course. As something inescapable, my character is part of my finitude. But it is not my whole self. As well as my character, I have my humanity, which is infinite, because I am capable of an infinite number of human virtues and vices, all of which take place in some sense outside myself. In Ricoeur's (1965a: 93) words, 'my humanity is my essential community with all that is human outside myself; that community makes every man my like'. However, humanity is not the opposite of character; rather, 'my character is that humanity seen . . . from a certain angle' (Ricoeur 1965a: 93). Thus my character is what makes me different from others who are like me: that others are like me, meanwhile, means that 'I do not aim at "my" personal idea of happiness and honour but happiness and honour *per se*' (Ricoeur 1965: 94). Character is that which I must have in order to have a point of view.

As for that happiness which man aims towards, there is again a disproportionate relationship between it and character, which comes out of the disproportion between finitude and the infinite. If character is finite (because it is unchanging and determined by the fact of my having been born), then happiness is an example of the infinite, or, as Ricoeur (1965a: 100) puts it in one of his more poetic moments, 'happiness is the horizon from every point of view'. Happiness is that which we all aim towards, regardless of the individual actions which might bring pleasure, or absence of pain, to individual characters. Character is 'the zero-point' of my 'field of orientation', while 'happiness is its infinite end' (Ricoeur 1965a: 104). In other words, whatever I aim at in life I must start from my having a character, and the ultimate goal of everything I do is happiness. My character is finite, and because happiness is happiness *per se* and not *my* happiness, it is infinite. It is this difference which leads to 'disproportion': 'no act gives happiness, but the encounters of our life which are most worthy of being called "events" indicate the direction of happiness' (Ricoeur 1965a: 104–5). We start from a position of misery – the opposite of happiness – because our birth is an event for others, not for ourselves, and so we start from a position of an absence of happiness, which must be acquired as we accumulate events.

How can we reconcile character with happiness? The answer is, through *respect*. Respect means acknowledging another person's *personality*. Personality is not the same as character: if character is pre-given, then personality is the humanity in a person. Humanity does not mean the collectivity of all people, but the human quality in each individual person. Being a human being consists in having a personality, which in turn consists of synthesising character with happiness, or reconciling my finitude with the infinite. I do this by recognising the personality of others, and this recognition is called 'respect'. Following the eighteenth-century German philosopher Immanuel Kant (1724–1804), Ricoeur calls respect a 'moral feeling', and this leads to a discussion of what constitutes *feelings* for man, the third moment at which man reveals himself to be fragile. Here, however, Ricoeur is making a daring move philosophically: he calls the movement of his discussion from consciousness to self-consciousness to feeling (or 'the heart') an 'advance' (Ricoeur 1965a: 124), whereas philosophers such as Kant thought that feelings were a kind of 'intuition', something we had to accept in philosophy without argument, but which the philosopher then moved away from.

FEELING

The pattern of Ricoeur's 'philosophy of feeling', though, is similar to that of the other two moments of fragility. He sees feeling as divided between two aspects: the *intentional* and the *affective*; however, this division is by no means a simple one, but is paradoxical and 'perplexing' (Ricoeur 1965a: 127). By 'intentional', Ricoeur means that feelings are feelings *of* something, such as the loveable or the hateful. But, as Ricoeur (1965a: 127) says, 'it is a very strange intentionality which on the one hand designates qualities felt *on* things, *on* persons, *on* the world and on the other hand manifests the way the self is inwardly affected'. In other words, a feeling *of* something, such as a feeling of love or happiness, also means a feeling *towards* something ('I love you') or *because of* something ('I am happy because of you'). Feelings, then, are directed outwards towards this other something, but they are also directed inwards towards me – they *affect* me (which is why they are called 'affects').

Philosophically, we might want to separate the intentions from the affects: this is what the 'phenomenological reduction' does in the realm of thinking, for example. But in the realm of feeling, the same manoeuvre is not possible: try to separate the object of the feeling from its inner affect and the object disappears along with it, and vice versa. If I love you, I cannot just say 'I love' without thinking of the 'you', and conversely I cannot think of 'you' without arousing a feeling of love within me.

This being so, we 'hesitate' (Ricoeur 1965a: 127) to call the things that our feelings are directed towards 'objects', since a subjective attitude is inextricably carried with them. Objects are *known* through the senses, through perception; feelings do not *know* objects in this sense. So, feelings are not directed straight at objects; they approach them indirectly. An object is perceived to be loveable, hateful, easy, difficult, etc. and then the 'things' (Ricoeur calls them 'quasi-objects') we have feelings of love, hate, ease and difficulty towards are the loveable, the hateful, the easy and the difficult, not the objects themselves. Hence 'I love you' means 'I love the loveable I perceive in you'.

So, how do we perceive that an object is loveable, hateful, etc.? We do so because we have what Ricoeur calls a *preferential outlook*. Bearing in mind all that has been said about the fact of our being born, and about character, we do not perceive anything neutrally, but we already, intuitively, have preferences: we prefer the loveable over the hateful, the pleasant over the unpleasant, etc. All of these preferences can be reduced to just one: we prefer the good over the bad. However, as intuitions 'good' and 'bad' here are not moral values: they are merely things we like and don't like. In other words, we simply *feel* the good to be good, the bad to be bad, etc. Likewise, if we think about objects as such rather than have feelings towards quasi-objects, the problem is the same: we have merely arrived at an intellectual judgement that something is good or bad. I cannot love the good merely by judging which objects are good and deciding to love them – to love is not a *decision* in that sense. So, if both *feeling* the good and the bad, and *knowing* the good and the bad, are inadequate by themselves, the only way to arrive at an adequate, *moral* understanding of the good and the bad is to synthesise feeling and knowing.

CONFLICT AND CREATIVITY

This leads Ricoeur to the conclusion (which happily confirms his working hypotheses) that '*conflict* is a function of man's most primordial constitution': this is a conflict within man between his self and his others, his character and his personality, his thinking and his feeling, etc. On the one hand Ricoeur prefers the latter of each of these pairings: other people, personality and fellow-feeling are all openings into the community of humanity, points at which the subjective self partakes of the qualities that all human beings have. On the other hand, he sees this inner conflict itself as not necessarily being a bad thing, since it leads to creativity. Ricoeur had ended *The Voluntary and the Involuntary* with the words 'To will is not to create'. It is our restlessness, the inherent insatiability of our desires, that drives us on as humanity and leads us to create a history for ourselves in a way the animals do not. Feeling 'assures me that I can "*continue my existence in*" the openness of thinking and of acting' (Ricoeur 1965a: 209). This assurance is a joyous affirmation, but it can only be understood by passing through its sad negation, which shows itself in our typically negative language: 'I need you' really means 'I do not have you', etc. This moment of negation, and the fact that it must be passed through in order to understand what has been affirmed, constitutes man's fallibility, his fault and his fragility. It is the point of insertion of evil into the world, but, more than that, it constitutes man's *capacity* for evil.

THE SYMBOLISM OF EVIL

Man makes a leap from being fallible to being already fallen by making an *avowal* of his capacity for evil. This avowal is expressed in '*symbols* of evil' (Ricoeur 1965a: 219). Ricoeur's remaining task is to describe, through what he calls a 'symbolics of evil', the way in which man is not only fallible, but fallen, 'to make the transition from the possibility of evil in man to its reality, from fallibility to fault' (Ricoeur 1967: 3).

A PHENOMENOLOGY OF CONFESSION

To make this transition from fallibility to fault, Ricoeur embarks on what he calls a 'phenomenology of confession', 're-enacting' the confession made by a religious consciousness in order to examine the experience from a philosophical point of view. There are two points to note about confession: that it is a linguistic phenomenon, and that evil does not become evil from a phenomenological point of view (i.e. from the point of view of an individual who commits evil) until at least the possibility of confessing it arises to consciousness. To put it the other way around, the possibility of confession is already contained within an evil deed. This being so, evil is known through its symbols, since the symbols provide the material out of which the confession is to be constructed.

DEFILEMENT

Ricoeur sees confession – our behaviour relating to fault – as arising from three sources: defilement, sin and guilt. Defilement is more basic than sin; it has its origins in notions of impurity. Defilement, says

Ricoeur (1967: 35), 'was never literally filthiness, dirtiness'; it has always been read symbolically, as 'ethical dread', the dread of the impure or of contamination. Dread of the impure is not a physical fear of getting dirty; already dread has been 'sublimated', carrying with it the fear of losing something essential to one's being, and consequently the need to face a threat. With this need comes a demand, 'the demand for just punishment' (Ricoeur 1967: 42). Just punishment does not only mean retribution for having made one dirty: it means removing the defilement and restoring the wronged party to a state of purity. Thus punishment should have a limit and an aim: the aim should be to restore the order that existed before the digression, and the limit should be reached when that aim is fulfilled.

The counterpart to the ethical dread of the impure is the ethical dread that one should be punished oneself. Ricoeur (1967: 45) is quite keen on the idea of punishment:

> The project of an education which would dispense with prohibition and punishment, and so with fear, is not only chimerical but harmful. Much is learned through fear and obedience – including the liberty which is inaccessible to fear.

This liberty is Christian love, and fear is necessary because we live in an imperfect world: 'because man never loves enough, it is not possible that the fear of not being loved in return should be abolished. Only *perfect* love casts out fear' (Ricoeur 1967: 45).

SIN

If the symbolism of defilement is 'archaic', then the symbolism of sin comes about once a society has a concept of God. If the counterpart of defilement is justice, the counterpart of sin is redemption. The symbols of defilement are positive, insofar as something is *added* to the subject who is defiled; the symbols of sin are negative insofar as they put the subject in a position of lacking something. Negative symbols of sin include the missed target, the tortuous road, the revolt and having gone astray. The difference between the symbols of sin and the symbols of defilement consists in the former 'not so much signify[ing] a harmful substance as a violated relation'; they suggest 'the idea of a relation broken off' (Ricoeur 1967: 74). They 'are analogies of the movement of existence considered as a whole' in that the sinner is he who has gone away from, or forgotten, God. This in turn leads to the idea of idolatry and the jealous God: *redemption* is a return to God.

GUILT

The third mode of confession, or of behaviour relating to fault, is guilt. The difference between guilt and sin or defilement is that guilt is subjective, whereas defilement and sin are, at least in part, objective. Defilement takes place through the intervention of an external body; sin is a shared, public symbolisation of fault; but guilt, meanwhile, interiorises fault: 'Guiltiness is never anything else than the anticipated chastisement itself, internalised and already weighing upon consciousness' (Ricoeur 1967: 101). If we realise that sin ought in justice to be punished, and if that realisation accompanies the sin itself, then guilt is *our* anticipation of punishment that accompanies *our own* sinful deeds. This constitutes what Ricoeur (1967: 102) calls 'a veritable revolution in the experience of evil', since 'what is primary is no longer the reality of defilement', but rather 'the evil use of liberty'. In other words, we have freedom to act and have abused that freedom, and the consciousness of this is experienced as a devaluing of ourselves.

Once this has been grasped, the next inevitable stage is to confess guilt – guilt is *truly* confessional in ways in which defilement and sin are not, in that in defilement I accuse another, in sin I am accused, but in guilt I accuse myself. This leads to a change of emphasis before God: in fact, God is not strictly necessary in order to feel guilt in the same way that He is necessary to a sense of sin, since in guilt it is what we call *conscience* that takes over from a jealous, punitive Almighty. What in turn is significant about this is that it introduces a sense of *measure* of evil. Sin is an absolute: in the eyes of God, something is either sinful, or it is not. But once we advance to guilt, we can see varying *degrees* of evil, measured according to the degree of guilt we feel towards our evil deeds. Guilt, moreover, marks a movement from the religious to the ethical, which is to say, from being answerable towards God to being answerable towards other people.

Ricoeur is not claiming that, once we have arrived at a concept of guilt, we can abandon God, since guilt can *only* be arrived at by the preceding two stages of defilement and sin, which retain a ghostly presence within the concept of guilt: in order to express itself, guilt must have 'recourse to the prior symbolism' (Ricoeur 1967: 152) of the two prior stages. Seen in this composite kind of way, defilement, sin and guilt become three elements of what Ricoeur (1967: 156) calls the 'servile will', 'the bad choice that binds itself'. Guilt is the ultimate expression of the free will that becomes unfree by binding itself to a bad choice.

MYTHS

But this is not the end of the story. In the second part of *The Symbolism of Evil*, Ricoeur (1967: 156) sets out to demonstrate that

> evil is not symmetrical with the good, wickedness is not something that replaces the goodness of a man; it is the staining, the darkening, the disfiguring of an innocence, a light, and a beauty that remain. However *radical* evil may be, it cannot be as *primordial* as goodness.

Ricoeur (1967: 306) does this by explaining – or, more precisely, by uncovering the hidden intentions behind – four different types of myth: the myth of the creation of the world, the myth of the 'tragic' vision of existence, the myth of the fallen man and the myth of the exiled soul.

According to Ricoeur, all creation myths, before telling of the creation of the world, tell of the creation of the divine. This is the most naïve of all of the types of myth, being as it is indebted to storytelling and sexual production: in essence, these myths are alternative answers to the question 'where did I come from?' The hidden intention of these myths is twofold: first, that whatever there is to say about the world is a result of its origin, and second, that evil is primordial, consisting of a disorder that is put to right by the order that is the world.

The tragic vision of existence, meanwhile, depends on a notion of a wicked God – Greek tragedy is the model here, although it is not unique to the Greeks. The elements of the tragic are blindness sent by the gods, the given portion, share or 'lot', and jealousy or immoderation: put them all together and we have the spectacle of a hero blinded to the consequences of exceeding his given lot through jealousy or rashness. And we should emphasise the spectacle: unlike the myth of creation, the tragic vision *is* a vision, being orientated towards watching a sight rather than hearing a story. The hidden intention, meanwhile, is of deliverance or purification, which comes to the object of the spectacle through his experience, and to the audience through witnessing it.

The third type of myth, that of the fall, is the 'Adamic' myth, 'the anthropological myth *par excellence*' (Ricoeur 1967: 232). Ricoeur is keen to note the difference between the Adamic myth and other myths of primordial man: the myth of Prometheus, for example, with which the myth of Adam is often compared, is closer to Greek tragedy in that it imputes the origin of evil to Zeus. (Prometheus stole fire – and, by extension, knowledge in general – from the gods and gave it to man, whom Zeus arbitrarily wished to destroy. As a punishment, Prometheus was impaled on a rock at the edge of the world. He is seen as the champion of mankind in the face of a tyrannical God.) What is special about the Adamic myth, meanwhile, is that it locates the origin of evil in man – this is why it is 'strictly anthropological' (Ricoeur 1967: 233), since there is no one else apart from man to blame for the evil that is in the world. In this respect the term 'myth of the fall' is not strictly correct, since a fall is usually accidental and brought about by an external factor. So, the first hidden intention of the myth of Adam is that he *sins* (according to the definition of 'sin' above) – he not so much falls, as goes astray. The second hidden intention is to separate the origin of evil from the origin of good: evil is *radical* (in the sense, say, of 'free radicals'), in that it exists as something that the evil doer himself brings into the world through his deeds.

All of this introduces a motif into the myth that is not present in the other two types – that of penitence. But penitence still means that there is something absolutely forbidden. (Evil is not absolutely forbidden, otherwise we would not be able to do it – evil is permitted by the fact of free will.) That something which is absolutely forbidden is 'a state of autonomy which would make man the creator of the distinction between good and evil' (Ricoeur 1967: 250). Man is free, but he is not autonomous: what constitutes evil is still decided by God. Moreover, another hidden intention of this myth is that 'sin does not *succeed* innocence' (Ricoeur 1967: 251); innocence can be seen as the absence of guilt, but can only be so seen from the perspective of sin. So, although we might be guilty subsequent to being innocent, we are *already* sinful at the time of being innocent: innocence means being innocent of our own sin. It is for this reason that these myths (as well as the myth of Adam himself Ricoeur includes that of Job and of Satan in Persian mythology) are typically characterised by a lapse of time in which temptation is dramatised. That time is, symbolically, the time in which sin as such gets caught up by *sins* (plural), particular sinful deeds which are going to lead to the realisation of one's sinfulness, and hence to guilt and penitence.

The fourth type of myth, that of the exiled soul, is the one whereby 'man understands himself as the *same* as his "soul" and "*other*" than his "body"' (Ricoeur 1967: 279); the example *par excellence* is Orpheus.

ORPHEUS

Orpheus of Thrace was a famous musician. His wife, Eurydice, trod on a serpent while fleeing from a would-be rapist, and died of the bite. Orpheus descended into Tartarus in an attempt to fetch her back. Through his music he so soothed the ferryman Charon, the dog Cerberus and the three Judges of the Dead, that he was allowed to restore Eurydice to the upper world, but on one condition: that he not look behind him till she was under the light of the sun. Guided by the sounds of his lyre, Eurydice followed Orpheus up the dark passage, but when Orpheus reached the sunlight he looked behind him, not realising that Eurydice had yet to emerge. Consequently, she was lost to him for ever.

The difference between this type of myth and that of Adam is that it makes the body an *eschatological force*, 'eschatology' being the theology of last things, such as death. In other words, in this myth the body dies and the soul continues. Various themes follow from this, the most important being that

> life and death alternate as two states: life comes from death and death comes from life, like waking and sleeping; the one may be the dream of the other, and each borrows its meaning from the other. Hence, the punishment is not only incarnation, but reincarnation; and so existence, under the sign of repetition, appears to be a perpetual backsliding.
>
> (Ricoeur 1967: 284)

Another theme is that of 'infernal punishment'. Although this theme is not wholly consistent with the one of alternation between death and life, nevertheless these two themes have a 'profound unity' (Ricoeur 1967: 285), in that 'life is a repetition of hell, as hell is a doublet of life'. This explains to believers in the myth why the 'terrifying spectacle' of the torments of history are presented to us, even though they are not ethical in the sense of justice being involved: history is littered with massacres, natural disasters etc., in which people go through great suffering despite being 'innocent'. The theme of alternation between this world and the next is more 'anthropological' than the theme of infernal punishment, in that it sees the soul as a window to the next world which can be seen through in this life, as in the experiences of 'dreams, ecstasies, love and death' (Ricoeur 1967: 286).

MYTHS IN MODERNITY

The Orphic myth is the most 'philosophical' of the myths, in that 'philosophy would not have tried to conceive the soul's identity with itself if the myth had not inspired it' (Ricoeur 1967: 289); moreover, it is the most recent of the myths to develop, being a significant feature of Greek civilisation and the myth on which Plato founded his philosophy. This most chronologically advanced form of mythology already carries within itself the possibility of escaping its own myth-ness, and becoming speculation – and speculation, unlike mythology, does not require symbolism. We moderns are living in a post-mythological, speculative age – we are 'children of criticism', as Ricoeur (1967: 306) puts it. But this does not mean that myths no longer have anything to say to us: 'we would not have interrogated them if they had not challenged us and if they could not address themselves to us' (Ricoeur 1967: 306). Nor are we, though, pure spectators of myths: we have memory and perspective, and so cannot address all four types of myth from a neutral position, 'regard[ing] everything with equal sympathy' (Ricoeur 1967: 306).

This being the case, Ricoeur identifies one type of myth as being 'pre-eminent' to us, and that is the Adamic myth. This is for three reasons, which all come down to our being, in the West, culturally Christian, or, in Ricoeur's own case, Christian in a more profound sense. The first reason is that 'the faith of the Christian believer is not concerned primarily with an interpretation of evil, its nature, its origin and its end; the Christian does not say: I believe in sin, but: I believe in the remission of sins; sin gets its full meaning only retrospectively' (Ricoeur 1967: 307). The second reason is that Christianity entails the Holy Spirit, which 'is not an arbitrary and absurd commandment', but a 'discernment': in addressing itself to my intelligence, it invites me to 'practice . . . the discernment of myths' (Ricoeur 1967: 308). In other words, it is an invitation to engage in precisely the sort of interpretation that Ricoeur's work consists of. For the Christian, the Holy Spirit

invites the Adamic myth not to be taken at face value, but to be interpreted. Third, 'the Adamic myth does not imply that the other myths
are purely and simply abolished' (Ricoeur 1967: 309); the Adamic
myth gives 'new life' to the other myths by appropriating them. Ricoeur
claims that there is a struggle among myths: on the one hand, the
Adamic myth wins the struggle, but on the other hand, it allows
the inner truths of the other myths to be understood in their varying
degrees. The other myths may be less true than the Adamic myth, but
they are by no means *un*true. Likewise, 'the myth of the fall needs those
other myths', so that the guilty man denounced by its God 'may also
appear as the victim of a mystery of iniquity which makes him deserving
of Pity as well as of Wrath' (Ricoeur 1967: 346).

SUMMARY

Ricoeur conceives of life as a dialectic between the will (the voluntary) and
the passions (the involuntary). A *phenomenological* investigation of the
will reveals it to be divided into three modes: to decide, to move the body,
and to consent. Each of these involves the opposite of the will, the involuntary, to some extent: to decide is motivated by reasons, to move the body is
subject to the unconscious and force of habit, and to consent is to subject
oneself to necessity. That each of these involuntary features are an intrinsic
part of the composition of the voluntary will, demonstrates that the Cartesian
cogito is an insufficient means of gaining self-knowledge, and incorrect in
its implication that there is a division between the soul, or mind and the
body. The mind cannot be imagined without a body, and thought is only
thought so long as thinking is done within a body. Once this is grasped,
thinking is no longer a self-sufficient activity, but dependent on what is
external to the mind. Human *existence* is the unity of the subjective
with the objective. The fact of our existence being dependent on a body
is a mystery that must be accepted in order to live, not a problem which
philosophy can solve.

So long as man has freedom to act, he is fallible. Fallibility comes from
the possibility of succumbing to the passions: since the passions come
from the body and the body is an intrinsic part of existence, the possibility of falling (i.e. of being evil) is inherent in man's constitution. The
extent of this possibility can be measured by the disproportion within man's

existence between the freedom to act and the necessity that constrains him to act in a certain way. There are three measures of this disproportion, which are three ways in which man is morally fragile: imagination, character and feeling. Each of these is a different way of relating to others: in imagination, I see myself as others see me; in character, I differentiate myself from the rest of humanity that is just like me; and in feeling I recognise the good and bad qualities of others (and, through having a 'preferential outlook', prefer the good). The imagination, character and feeling must be synthesised with the mind to form a whole person, and thus a person with moral status. This conflict between the non-intellectual and the intellectual is what is creative about humanity, but it is also what allows in the possibility of evil, since it is through imagination, character and feeling that we are most likely to err in going against our better judgement or 'preferential outlook'.

This explains why man is *fallible*; why he is *fallen* is explained by the hidden intentions behind myths, that still colour our 'preferential outlook' today. The route from fallibility to fallenness is a route from defilement through sin to guilt, which is a route from violation by an external force, through the possibility of being punished for committing a violation, to the interiorisation of the punishment as conscience. This route is reproduced in the historical development of myths. Creation myths claim that evil is primordial; they are replaced by a tragic vision of the world, which claims that the gods are evil. This myth in turn is superseded by the myths of Adam and of Orpheus. The Adamic myth attributes evil to man's own fault, and the Orphic myth gives the promise of an eternal soul. Although the Orphic myth is the most intellectual, the Adamic myth is the most significant, since it is the one which embodies the symbols of sin and guilt as opposed to defilement. Moreover, it invites itself to be interpreted, and so is an allegory that, through constant reinterpretation, remains pertinent throughout history as a lesson in the unchanging nature of the human condition.

2

HERMENEUTICS

Hermeneutics is the theory for which Ricoeur is most celebrated. In the 1960s, beginning with *The Symbolism of Evil*, Ricoeur sees hermeneutics merely as a method of interpreting symbols. However, he subsequently refines hermeneutics into a theory of interpreting discourse as a whole, including, but not confined to, the symbols which any discourse contains. Essentially, hermeneutics becomes a theory of text, which takes texts as its starting point, but ultimately comes to see the world as textual, insofar as human existence is expressed through discourse, and discourse is the invitation humans make to one another to be interpreted.

INTERPRETATION OF SYMBOLS

Ricoeur's hermeneutics brackets off *semantic* meaning in texts in order to focus on *symbolic* meaning: his slogan is 'the symbol gives rise to thought' (Ricoeur 1967: 352). The distinction here is between what a text *says* and what it *shows*. Take the sentence '2 + 2 = 4'. This is a proposition which is *verifiable*: I can test whether it is true or false (and, in fact, this particular proposition is always true). This truth-value is the sentence's *semantic meaning*. But in George Orwell's novel *Nineteen Eighty-Four*, the sentence '2 + 2 = 4' not only has *semantic* meaning, but also a range of *symbolic* meanings to do with freedom, the rights of the individual etc. Notice how (i) the symbolic meaning is quite independent of the semantic meaning – in the novel, the issue is about the right to assert that $2 + 2 = 4$, not about testing whether it is true or not; and (ii) that in order to arrive at the symbolic meaning, we have to look at the whole textual context in which the sentence is situated – by contrast to the semantic meaning, the symbolic meaning is not derivable from the sentence in isolation. It is for this reason that Ricoeur is interested in symbolic meanings – they reach out beyond the language in which they are couched to the broader text. Through its symbolic meanings, it is the text as a whole that tells us some truth about the world. The truth-value of '$2 + 2 = 4$' is timeless, and will be so regardless of whether or not there are any humans around to appreciate it. But the truths revealed by symbolic meanings are *human* truths, telling us something about life as lived through human experience.

According to Ricoeur in *The Symbolism of Evil*, in modernity we have forgotten the meanings of symbols. One of the tasks of hermeneutics is to forget the forgetting, and to restore the original meanings of symbols. In some ways, hermeneutics has always existed before it was given that name in the nineteenth century, or its modern meaning by Ricoeur, in that symbols always already carry with them an invitation to be interpreted. But modern hermeneutics is different from the type of interpretation that an ancient seer would give to dreams, for example, in that it must be part of the tradition of *critical* thought. Hermeneutics must be philosophical, insofar as it must not only explain what the allegorical meaning of a symbol is (that a serpent symbol is an allegory of evil, for example), but also *why* any particular symbol functions in any particular allegorical manner (in our example, not only why it is a *serpent* that should be an allegory of evil, but also why that particular allegorical meaning should be placed within whatever myth it is to be found). However, Ricoeur does not see these two tasks of hermeneutics – of restoring meanings to symbols and of criticising them – as being contradictory, but as complementary:

> The dissolution of the myth as explanation is the necessary way to the restoration of the myth as symbol. Thus, the time of restoration is not a different time from that of criticism; we are in every way children of criticism, and we seek to go beyond criticism by means of criticism, by a criticism that is no longer reductive but restorative.
>
> (Ricoeur 1967: 350)

The result is a 'creative interpretation, an interpretation that would respect the original enigma of symbols, let itself be taught by this enigma, but, with that as a start, bring out the meaning' (Ricoeur 1974: 300). In other words, hermeneutics respects the priority of meaning *within* symbols, rather than assuming that there has already been a philosophy lying behind symbols which their symbolic nature, or the myths in which symbols are couched, have set out to veil.

LANGUAGE AND TEXTS

The task of hermeneutics is to discover meaning. As in most of philosophy, 'meaning' here means the meaning of life or, at least, meaning *in* life. But hermeneutics is based on a view of the world that sees language as the medium through which not only meanings (plural) are conveyed, but also Meaning in this grander, philosophical sense. But hermeneutics is not really concerned with language in the same way that linguistics is, or even that philosophy of language is: broadly speaking, linguistics seeks to describe language, and philosophy of language seeks to explain the conditions under which language can operate, have meaning and be truthful. Hermeneutics is not interested in linguistic description, nor is it interested in traditional semantics (theory of meaning). Rather, the hermeneuticist sees the world related to the individual through the mediation of texts. I understand the world not directly, but through texts – and this means through texts seen as wholes, not as individual linguistic units combined together. This does not mean that pre-literate cultures, or illiterate people, cannot or do not understand the world – as a method, hermeneutics is just as capable of applying itself to the myths of oral cultures as it is to the documents of written cultures. But Ricoeur himself has a predilection for written texts, and tends to examine oral discourse as if it were written. This is because 'writing tears itself free of the limits of face-to-face dialogue' (Ricoeur 1991a: 17): unlike speech, it is autonomous 'in relation to the speaker's intention, to its reception by its original audience, and to the economic, social, and cultural circumstances of its production'. If hermeneutics is not interested in these things, what, then, is its task?

> It is ... to seek in the text itself, on the one hand, the internal dynamic that governs the structuring of the work and, on the other hand, the power that the work possesses to project itself outside itself and to give birth to a world that

would truly be the 'thing' referred to by the text. This internal dynamic and external projection constitute what I call the work of the text. It is the task of hermeneutics to reconstruct this twofold work.

(Ricoeur 1991a: 17–18)

This internal dynamic and external projection of texts is, according to Ricoeur, owing to their *intentionality* – the fact that texts (i) don't just say things, but carry with them a force of belief in what is being said (the internal dynamic); and (ii) say things *to somebody*, with the intention of affecting the reader (the external projection).

INTENTIONAL MEANING

For Ricoeur, something only means if it is imbued with what Husserl called *Bedeutungsintention*, 'meaning-intention' – in other words, if someone intended the discourse he is examining to be meaningful to someone perceiving it. We have seen how, in his interpretation of myths, Ricoeur is interested in their hidden intentions – in the *intentional* meaning of texts. Here we must pause to point out that the intentional meaning is *not* the same as 'what the author intended': indeed, in *The Symbolism of Evil* Ricoeur is concerned with texts which do not have an 'author' in the received sense, such as myths or the Bible. Hermeneutics, rather, seeks to uncover the *mode of intentionality* that accompanies the text, be it belief, repentance, remorse or whatever. These are 'objective' modes insofar as they must be what motivates the meanings of texts regardless of whoever wrote them, so long as that person is part of a culture, and they must mean those things to *us*, so long as we are part of that culture too. In the myth of Adam, for example, the themes of jealousy, temptation, desire, punishment and remorse (each leading to the other) are a universal constant so long as human nature is a universal constant, and regardless of whether one 'believes' the myth in either a historical ('this really happened') or religious ('this is the word of God') sense.

UNDERSTANDING

The goal of hermeneutics is understanding. Hermeneutics is based on the premise that texts say something not only about themselves, but also about the world at large. So, by reading texts in a hermeneutic way, we

INTENTIONALITY

Intentionality as a concept was first posited by the philosopher Franz Brentano (1838–1917), but it was developed by his pupil Edmund Husserl (1859–1938) in his *Logical Investigations* (1900). If, as according to Husserl, consciousness is always consciousness *of* something, then thinking is always thinking *of* something: I don't just think in the abstract, but I think *that* something is the case. Moreover, if I *think* that something is the case, I might also believe, consider, opine, judge, hope etc. that it is the case. Each of these ways of thinking is an *intentional state*; I have an *intentional attitude* towards the world around me. This possession of an intentional state or attitude is called 'intentionality'. Some sign systems can signify without being meaningful in this way – without, that is, being 'motivated' by an utterer's or an author's *Bedeutungsintention* (= 'meaning-intention'). Husserl's own example is the Martian 'canals', which signify that there has been intelligent life on Mars. (The fact that this is a *false* signification, since we now know that there has never been intelligent life on Mars, is irrelevant.) The creators of the Martian canals, had they existed, would not have built the canals to show earthlings that they were intelligent – they would have built them to get from Zig to Zag. That Martians were intelligent is merely something we infer (falsely, as it happens) from the existence of 'canals' on Mars. As Husserl says, the canals 'mean' only in the sense of indicating, and lack 'full' or *intended* meaning. More recent philosophers such as John Searle (b. 1932) have pointed out that the sentences constructed by computers also lack intentionality: a computer cannot *believe* (or disbelieve) the statements it makes. Thus intentionality has become a very important concept in philosophy, since it is held to be what distinguishes us as human, and there is an ongoing debate as to whether some or any of the animals are capable of attaching intentionality to their 'language'.

come to a greater understanding of the world. In his essay 'Existence and Hermeneutics' (1965), Ricoeur says that there is a short route and a long route to this understanding. The short route is the one taken by the philosopher Martin Heidegger (1889–1976) and his followers. They reject the Cartesian *cogito* altogether, in favour of an 'ontology of understanding'. Ontology is discourse about being. An ontology of understanding holds that man is *already* 'a self-interpreting animal', as Charles Taylor (1985: 45) puts it, so that the *cogito* says nothing new, because I must *already* understand what it means in order to assert it. The ontologist then sets about answering the question: 'What kind of being is it whose being consists of understanding?' (Ricoeur 1974: 6).

Heidegger's work was a radical development of that of his teacher, Husserl – so much so, that Husserl found Heidegger's ontological philosophy unrecognisable as the phenomenology he had invented. Ricoeur prefers Husserl's long phenomenological route, rather than Heidegger's short ontological route, to understanding. While acknowledging the usefulness of Heidegger, Ricoeur goes back to the phenomenological tradition of Husserl in his hermeneutics. But if the goal of both of these philosophical traditions – the ontological, as represented by Heidegger, and phenomenological, as represented by Husserl – is the same, namely *understanding*, then what is the point of taking the long route when the short route will do? The answer, for Ricoeur, is that the route itself is worthwhile in its own right. The route to

MARTIN HEIDEGGER (1889–1976)

Martin Heidegger's *Being and Time* (1927) represented a revolution in modern philosophy. Heidegger was interested in the *ontological* question, i.e. the question of being: what is being, and what does it mean to have being? For Heidegger, man is unique in being the entity for which the question of being is an issue for it. Man is the only animal aware of its own being – aware that it *has* being rather than merely being – and this having-being is what man must take as presupposed before being able to advance any question of knowledge. For this reason Heidegger rejects Descartes' search for an answer to the question 'What can I know?' – Heidegger's project is to 'destroy' Western metaphysics – in favour of an investigation into the nature of the kind of being – man – who is capable of being aware of his own being. Heidegger gives the name *Dasein* to man in his awareness of his own being: *Dasein* means 'being-there', an entity that can be designated as having being, but which is also already thrown into the situation of having being as something which must be presupposed. Heidegger calls his project an *existential analytic of Dasein*, in other words, an exercise in analysing the being of man from the standpoint of taking existence as a pre-given. In this he has much in common with the existentialists whom he influenced, although he reached entirely different conclusions from them regarding the relationship of man to the world at large.

understanding is part of the constitution of understanding. The hermen-euticist, like the phenomenologist before him, tries to *resolve* problems rather than *dissolve* them.

THE HERMENEUTIC CIRCLE

The short route is short because it rejects all methodology to get straight to the question of being; and the kind of being (man) who is aware of his own being through understanding. The long route is long because it follows the *hermeneutic circle* around its circumference back to the same point, rather than simply staying put. The hermeneutic circle is a problem first described by Heidegger in his *Being and Time* (1927). There he points out that, as a consequence of understanding of existence being dependent on understanding of the world and vice versa, 'any inter-pretation which is to contribute understanding, must already have understood what is to be interpreted' (Heidegger 1962: 194). This is a problem for scientific knowledge: how can we advance knowledge if the X we are trying to prove already presupposes X? Science turns this circle into a virtuous one by means of the *working hypothesis*, by which X is supposed for the sake of argument, and then the supposition is tested by empirical means. The case is different with historiography (writing about history). Many people today would take it for granted that history is not a science, since after all history departments tend to be found in Arts or Humanities faculties. But Heidegger is writing quite close in time to Karl Marx (1818–83) and his followers, who claimed history to be a predictable series of events determined by the 'scientific' laws of class struggle. According to Heidegger, on the contrary, what happens in historical events cannot be tested by empirical means – their 'truth' is dependent on the subjective standpoint of the observer. One historian's creation of Israel is another's destruction of Palestine, for example – the interpretation of the event is already contained in its description. In historiography, then, the hermeneutic circle would be a vicious circle, and for Heidegger this means that history cannot be a science, since historiography is incapable of uncovering objective truth.

Ricoeur's statement of the hermeneutic circle is a little different from Heidegger's: 'We must understand in order to believe, but we must believe in order to understand' (Ricoeur 1967: 351). The circle can also be expressed in a different way: 'hermeneutics proceeds from a prior understanding of the very thing that it tries to understand by interpreting it' (Ricoeur 1967: 352). Like Heidegger, however, Ricoeur does not see this as a vicious circle, but as 'a living and stimulating circle'. In doing hermeneutics, each half of the equation – understanding to believe and believing to understand – should seek kinship with the other, 'a kinship of thought with what life aims at' (Ricoeur 1967: 352). In such a way, hermeneutics understands itself, and its circularity is itself a gift which enables the hemeneut to 'communicate with the sacred by making explicit the prior understanding that gives life to the interpretation' (Ricoeur 1967: 352). Hermeneutics is therefore in some sense a rediscovery of the naïvety, whereby symbols were originally believed immediately.

THE WAGER

Thus far hermeneutics only constitutes a re-enactment of the process of believing – it does not constitute belief as such, which can only be arrived at by thought. If the hermeneutic circle is the 'gift' of 'the symbol gives rise to thought', then we must proceed to the 'thought'. To do this we must break the hermeneutic circle and get beyond it. This is achieved 'by transforming it into a *wager*' (Ricoeur 1967: 355). The wager is

> that I shall have a better understanding of man and of the bond between the being of man and the being of all beings if I follow the *indication* of symbolic thought. That wager then becomes the task of *verifying* my wager and saturating it, so to speak, with intelligibility. In return, the task transforms my wager: in betting *on* the significance of the symbolic world, I bet at the same time *that* my wager will be restored to me in power of reflection, in coherent discourse.
> (Ricoeur 1967: 355)

Ricoeur's hermeneutics, then, 'starts from symbols and endeavours to promote the meaning, to form it, by a creative interpretation' (Ricoeur 1967: 355).

So, to do hermeneutics we must combine Husserl's *phenomenological* way of looking at the world (bracketing off all that is non-essential to the phenomenon itself when contemplating it) with the *intentional* theory of meaning (that meaning is motivated by an intentional attitude). Hermeneutics reads meanings in an essential way. In other words, it looks at the symbols in texts as phenomena, and in so doing uncovers the intentional attitude that makes them meaningful.

DISTANCIATION

Ricoeur was working on *The Symbolism of Evil* too soon to assimilate Hans-Georg Gadamer's *Truth and Method*, which was also published in 1960. On becoming acquainted with Gadamer's work, Ricoeur realises that the interpretation of symbols, while a necessary part of hermeneutics, is not sufficient in itself, and he therefore enhances and refines his theory of hermeneutics into a theory of not just symbols within texts, but a theory of texts as such, of *textuality*.

HANS-GEORG GADAMER (1900–2002)

Gadamer's monumental *Truth and Method* (1960) represents the first attempt to develop a fully fledged 'hermeneutics' in the modern sense. Gadamer's hermeneutics are concerned with uncovering the deeper truths of human life than are to be found using scientific method. He bases revelation of such truths first on aesthetic experience (the experience of works of art), and from this broadens the enquiry into experience as such. Experience is opposed to philosophy, since the latter is speculative, whereas the former entails engagement with a *tradition* through which artefacts are understood. *Language* is the medium of this understanding; that man is the being who speaks is what makes him the being who is able to achieve 'historical self-consciousness'. This is done through hermeneutics: works of art carry with them an invitation to be interpreted, not in an 'objective' way, but as a 'conversation' between those whom it touches. It is this conversation itself which constitutes the 'true' meaning of art, and by extension of life, for Gadamer.

The most important of Gadamer's ideas to influence Ricoeur is that of *distanciation*. Distanciation is the effect of being made *distant* from the producer of a text and the cultural conditions under which he or she wrote. This is specifically a textual effect, since it is the ability of a text to endure through history (so that the reader is separated from the author in both space and time) that causes it. (Ricoeur concedes that *any* form of discourse has the potential to produce distanciation, but it is text that advances distanciation beyond a merely 'primitive' level.) Whereas Gadamer found distanciation 'alienating', however, Ricoeur (1991a: 76) finds it 'positive and productive'. For him, text 'displays a fundamental characteristic of the very historicity of human experience, namely that it is communication in and through distance'.

HISTORICITY

The fact of something being historical; 'historicalness': 'historic quality or character (opposed to legendary or fictitious)' (*Oxford English Dictionary*).

Text becomes distanciating through a number of 'dialectical' stages ('dialectical' in the sense that each stage incorporates the previous). The first stage is the realisation of language as discourse within text. Just as phenomenologists like Husserl say that consciousness is always consciousness *of* something, so Ricoeur claims that language is always language *about* something. As soon as language is spoken, it becomes an event – it becomes *discourse*. Language is merely a system, but uttering discourse locates language in the time of the utterance. Moreover, discourse says something more than mere language – it tells us who is speaking, and who is spoken to. In short, the event of discourse consists of the realisation of our linguistic competence in performance. The difference between language and discourse can be illustrated by comparing two newspaper headlines: *General Belgrano Sunk* and *Gotcha!* The second contains fewer words, but is more discursive, and thus richer in meaning: it has a double addressee (the readers of the newspapers and the 'cha', those who were sunk), and it belies a strongly ideological attitude which it assumes its readers share (this is a victory of 'us' over 'them'), all of which is made possible by, and is only understandable through, a specific historical event located at a specific time (the sinking of the Argentinian ship *General Belgrano* by British forces during the Falklands War of 1982).

The second dialectical stage is when discourse becomes a structured work: 'Just as language, by being actualised as discourse, surpasses itself as system and realises itself as event, so too discourse, by entering the process of understanding, surpasses itself as event and becomes meaning' (Ricoeur 1991a: 78). A work carries more meaning than mere discourse, just as discourse carries more meaning than mere language. A work is (usually) longer than just one sentence, and so the *combination* of sentences has meaning in addition to each individual sentence. Also, a work is *composed*, which means both that it belongs to a genre (story, poetry, essay, etc.), and that it has a *style*. Moreover, a work in this sense of a piece of discourse which is composed, belongs to a genre and has a style is, according to Ricoeur, always a *text*. Textuality (what 'being a text' consists of) is doubly distanciating: it distances the work from its means of production, and it distances it from an audience. The text can be liberated from the psychological 'intentions' of its author and from the sociological conditions prevailing at the time of writing; moreover, it can be read not just by those to whom it is addressed, but by anyone who can read. Ricoeur finds this 'autonomy' of the text liberating: freed from these constraints, the text creates its own world. It is then up to the reader to inhabit that world, finding within it situations which explain his or her own situation: 'What must be interpreted in a text is a *proposed world* which I could inhabit and wherein I could project one of my ownmost possibilities. That is what I call the world of the text, the world proper to *this* unique text' (Ricoeur 1991a: 86).

This world of the text is the means by which the reader attains self-understanding, and the passage to this constitutes the fourth dialectical movement. The reader attains self-understanding by *appropriating* the work, which she can do through the distanciating effect of writing that has divorced the work from the author's intention: 'thanks to distanciation by writing, appropriation no longer has any trace of affective affinity with the intention of an author' (Ricoeur 1991a: 87). Although he does not mention him by name, clearly at this point Ricoeur's thinking coincides quite closely with that of the French cultural theorist and critic Roland Barthes (1915–80), who in a celebrated essay entitled 'The Death of the Author' (1966), claimed that 'a text is made of multiple writings, drawn from many cultures and entering into mutual relations of dialogue, parody, contestation, but there is one place where this multiplicity is focused and that place is the reader, not, as was hitherto said, the author' (Barthes 1977: 148). This affinity with Barthes is made more explicit in Ricoeur's short book *Interpretation Theory: Discourse and the Surplus of Meaning* (1976), in which he points out that at a certain time in human history, writing ceases to be 'merely the fixation of a previous oral discourse', and instead 'human thought [is] directly brought to writing without the intermediary stage of spoken language' (Ricoeur 1976: 28). Once we have 'written discourse', or 'inscription' in this sense, 'the author's intention and the meaning of the text cease to coincide' (Ricoeur 1976: 29); the text thus becomes 'semantically autonomous' from the point of view of its interpreter or reader.

While Gadamer finds the historical distance between the reader of a text and its author alienating, because it makes understanding the work more difficult, Ricoeur finds it liberating, because it enables the reader to understand herself through the mediation of the work *itself*, regardless of what its author intended. This idea leads Ricoeur (1991a: 88) to the paradoxical proposition that 'As reader, I find myself only by losing myself.' But we have all had the experience of 'losing ourselves' in a good book. In this experience, says Ricoeur, we 'expose' ourselves to the text, and enter into 'the world of the work'. We do not impose our understanding on the text, but rather let the text increase our understanding of life, which we do once we have put the book down. Taking seriously Heidegger's assertion that man is *primarily* an interpreting being, Ricoeur (1991a: 88) claims that 'to understand is to understand oneself in front of the text'. To read, then, is to do hermeneutics, and to do hermeneutics is to understand ourselves – to understand, among other things, that our being is such that it can only be fulfilled by doing hermeneutics. This circular argument is yet another variation of the hermeneutic circle, but its circularity does not make it pointless, unless we want to say that life is pointless – it is what we *do* in life, insofar as we are constantly interpreting the world around us in order to understand that our *raison d'être* is to interpret the world around us in order to understand it. It is the constant renewal of this circular journey, with all its imaginative variations on the theme, that makes life worthwhile.

SUMMARY

Ricoeur's practice in *The Symbolism of Evil* involves the *symbolic* interpretation of texts – interpreting not only what the individual sentences in the texts mean in a literal sense, but also what the whole text means above and beyond the sum of its parts. The meanings revealed by this kind of interpretation are the text's *intentional* meanings, 'intentional' to be taken in a special philosophical sense (quite independent of 'the author's intention') that the text is motivated by an attitude such as belief. The *hermeneutic circle* – that I must believe in order to understand but I must understand in order to believe – becomes a virtuous circle when I make the wager that my understanding will confirm my belief and vice versa.

In his essays written subsequent to *The Symbolism of Evil*, Ricoeur develops hermeneutics as a *phenomenological* philosophy, in that it suspends judgement about what I can know about the world through direct perception, in order to explore the routes of understanding the world. For Ricoeur, the main route to understanding the world is by reading it as if it

were a text, or, at least, reading texts is the best way to come to an understanding of the world. This is owing to the *distanciating* effect of *textuality*,
which is a positive force insofar as it allows the critical distance of *historicity*
between the reader and the text's means of production. Interpreting texts –
doing hermeneutics – is the route to self-understanding as a human being,
because being historical – having historicity – is a specifically human trait.
Texts propose a world which readers appropriate to understand their own
world, and consequently to understand themselves. Texts are the medium
through which readers arrive at self-understanding; they are the bridge
between the subjectivity of the self and the objectivity of the world.

3

PSYCHOANALYSIS

Ricoeur's work on psychoanalysis immediately succeeds *The Symbolism of Evil*, the final part of *Philosophy of the Will*. It consists principally of his monumental *Freud and Philosophy*, supplemented by various articles published during the 1960s, most of which are collected in *The Conflict of Interpretations* (1969). In writing of psychoanalysis, Ricoeur is concerned almost exclusively with the works of its founder, Sigmund Freud (1856–1939). His interest stems from the fact that, like hermeneutics, psychoanalysis is a method of interpretation, and, moreover, it is *symbols* which form the basis of the interpretations in both disciplines. These similarities notwithstanding, on the face of it it would appear that psychoanalysis and hermeneutics have completely opposing views of human life. It is Ricoeur's task to dig beneath this superficial appearance, and reveal the hidden affinity between psychoanalysis and hermeneutics.

PSYCHOANALYSIS VERSUS HERMENEUTICS

There are a number of differences between psychoanalysis and hermeneutics, which make it appear that Freud is an odd choice for Ricoeur to study, especially if his study is to be a sympathetic one. First, as Ricoeur (1970: 17) points out, Freud's theory of interpretation is one of suspicion: in dreams, for example, the unconscious is held to be the agent of cunning ruses, which it is the task of the patient, aided by the analyst, to decipher. The dream language, according to Freud, is a language of distortion, and it is so because the unconscious wishes to repress material, which in effect means to hide material from the conscious mind. For Ricoeur, meanwhile, as we have seen in his

SIGMUND FREUD

Freud's first major work, and arguably his most significant, was *The Interpretation of Dreams* (1899). Here Freud explains dreams as a kind of symbolism, a series of 'rebuses'. A rebus is a picture puzzle requiring a double work of translation: first from one code to another, and then within the second code. Hence, for example, a beer advertisement in the 1970s showed an enormous shin with a ladder up it, adjacent to a tin can. The first translation is from pictorial code to linguistic: 'high knee can'. The second translation is within the linguistic code: 'Heineken'. In dreaming, the 'dream work' performs this work of interpretation in reverse, in order to hide, or repress, the truth from the conscious mind. The truth, or real meaning, is unconscious.

In subsequent works Freud goes on to explain that the reason this material is repressed is that it is always at heart sexual, and derives from the answer to the child's question 'Where did I come from?', which is found in the 'primal scene', the real or (usually) imagined image of parental intercourse. Becoming aware, for the child, means becoming aware that he is not the only object of his mother's affections; his true desire is to displace the father in order to regain his 'rightful' place. This complex (called the 'Oedipus' complex after the character in Sophocles' play, who kills his father and marries his mother) is seen by Freud as determining the whole of human existence: most people successfully reconcile themselves to it, but the neurotic has failed to complete this work of reconciliation.

In later works still (especially in his *New Introductory Lectures on Psychoanalysis*, 1932), Freud develops a 'topography' of the psyche, in three parts: the id, the Ego and the super-ego. The id is what in the earlier work used to be called 'unconscious'; it is the unadulterated collection of primitive desires that have been forgotten by the conscious mind because they are repressed. The Ego is the conscious mind, sandwiched between the id and the super-ego. The super-ego is the conscience, which acts as a brake on the Ego by doing the work of repressing the id. Occasionally the id will out, however, as it does in dreams, jokes or flashes of wit.

treatment of myths, discourse does not intend to deceive. The language of myths may be a symbolic one, and that language may thus be constructed to hide the intention of the myth, but nevertheless the intention of the myth itself intends to be discovered. The myth invites interpretation – invites what is hidden to be discovered – whereas, according to Freud, the language of the unconscious, such as that to be found in dreams, is designed with the intention of never disclosing its true meaning. The psychoanalyst is therefore suspicious, uncovering what wishes to remain hidden, and suspecting language of attempting to deflect him from that path. The hermeneuticist, on the other hand, uncovers what wishes to be uncovered, and has faith in the veracity of language to lead towards what it really means.

A second distinction between Freudian psychoanalysis and Ricoeur's version of hermeneutics is that the former leads to atheism, whereas the latter is an expression of Christian belief. According to psychoanalysis, the conscience is a function of the super-ego, an agency of repression which instructs the mind to present a socially acceptable face to the world, and which helps to perform the work of burying precisely the kind of primal material which the psychoanalyst, through his analysis, seeks to uncover. In this way, 'conscience' becomes merely the name of that which is socially acceptable, and the only motive that the selfish mind has for obeying it – deny it as one might – is to conform to the dictates of society. This has the effect of relativising and internalising morality: whatever is good or bad is so because a society at any given time thinks it is good or bad, and it is up to the individual's judgement whether he is conforming to this morality or not, or even whether he should conform to it or not. There is no external, absolute moral standard by which good and evil may be measured; instead, 'good' and 'evil' are reduced to 'acceptable behaviour' and 'unacceptable behaviour' respectively. All of this is entirely inconsistent with Ricoeur's thinking, as shown in his work throughout *The Voluntary and the Involuntary* and subsequently. For Ricoeur, as we have seen, evil is real and is timelessly so, even if it is the case that evil comes from man's consciousness, and is not an external force acting upon him. Moreover, evil is not a direct counterpart to good, and so therefore cannot belong to the same *scale* of moral behaviour. While Ricoeur holds that man has a natural predisposition towards the good, Freud implies that we are naturally predisposed towards what we call 'evil' (but which Freud himself calls 'nature'). While for Ricoeur evil is something we admit into our hearts at the moments when we are most vulnerable, the moments when we allow ourselves to be guided by our passions, the implication of Freud's thinking on the other hand is that the world would be a better place if everyone allowed themselves openly to be guided by their passions. For psychoanalysis, 'fault' lies in the repression of those passions by polite society.

The third manner in which psychoanalysis appears incompatible with hermeneutics is that the latter is a version, or development, of phenomenology. Phenomenology is a philosophy of consciousness; psychoanalysis, meanwhile, takes the unconscious as its object of study. One of Ricoeur's developments of Cartesianism is to do away with dualism: instead of treating the mind as separable from the body, Ricoeur shares the phenomenological (and Christian existentialist) view that it is impossible for the mind to think of itself other than through the mediation of the body. Yet nevertheless, in making this claim, the phenomenologist does not go so far as to say that there is an unconscious, a part of the mind that exists and yet is unknown. There are thoughts which may be forgotten, it is true, but these thoughts can be recalled by the operation of the will. The fact that sometimes we cannot recall something we wish to is not a sign of repression, but of simple lapse of memory in the ordinary sense. That there should be an *agency* or *system* of the mind, which the mind itself is not aware of, controlling the mind and selecting which memories to make available to consciousness and which to suppress, is inconsistent with phenomenology's search for Cartesian certainty. What use would the Cartesian *cogito* – 'I think therefore I am' – be, if the 'I think' part of it did not designate all of my thinking, but only the parts of it that I am aware of? Freud would want to claim that that other part of the mind, the 'id' or 'it', thinks too. If that were the case, then the id would also have a claim to existence. But that would compromise the existence of the utterer of the *cogito*, who in saying 'I think therefore I am' wants to claim that he *is* as a totality – not that he is only in part. In fact, Freud (1973: 112) replaces the Cartesian *cogito* by the formula 'Where id was, there Ego shall be', which removes the present-tense 'am' from the formula altogether. The Ego, for Freud, never can with certainty say 'I *am*'. The subject – the person who says 'I' – is never quite identical with himself.

PSYCHOANALYSIS AS A HERMENEUTICS

Despite these enormous differences between the ways in which psycho-analysis and hermeneutics (and its predecessor, phenomenology) see the world, Ricoeur sets out to perform a *sympathetic* critique of Freud, one that, while highlighting certain shortcomings in psychoanalysis, never-theless maintains Freud's place as a major figure in the history of thought. To do this, Ricoeur first draws analogies, or points of contact and similarity, between psychoanalysis and hermeneutics. The point of this is not to gloss over their differences, but rather to show that psycho-analysis and hermeneutics approach the same truth, albeit in different ways and through differing routes.

The first similarity between psychoanalysis and hermeneutics is that they are both, in part, concerned with experiences of the sacred. Freud, for his part, wrote not only about the case studies of individual patients, but also about the 'psychopathology of everyday life', and in these writings his interest in anthropology, and particularly in how people experience religion, comes to the fore. Hermeneutics, meanwhile, philosophically comes out of phenomenology, but as an experience of reading comes out of 'biblical hermeneutics', the tradition of Bible interpretation. More fundamentally, the 'texts' that both psychoanalysis and hermeneutics deal with – the patient's discourse in the one case, and texts in the literal sense (but including myths, etc.) in the other – can be viewed as modes of confession. It has often been said that psycho-analysis is like secular confession, whereas hermeneutics (at least as practised by Ricoeur) is also concerned with the analysis of the fault in the human condition.

This brings us to a more general sense in which psychoanalysis and hermeneutics are aligned. They are both means of interpretation. It is Ricoeur's contention that psychoanalysis is a mode of hermeneutics. Despite the difference that psychoanalysis is suspicious of the discourse of the patient while hermeneutics has faith in the discourse of the text, both have the aim of discovering, or uncovering, a hidden inten-tion. Moreover, the aim of performing this task is the same – to make the world a better place. This is more than a 'Miss World' platitude. Most kinds of reading, from reading a magazine in the bath to doing literary criticism, are done for their own sakes, or as ends in themselves. But in both psychoanalysis and hermeneutics, the aim of the task is not merely to *explain* what is being read, but also to prompt action.

Psychoanalysis tells the patient how to act upon the truth of the revealed hidden meaning of the unconscious; hermeneutics finds in the hidden intentions of its texts instructions on how to behave in the world, ethically and politically. Another way of stating the same similarity is to say that both psychoanalysis and hermeneutics are not quite philosophy. They are *informed* by philosophy, but they are more practical than philosophy, being ways of interpreting, and suggestions of how to act upon the knowledge revealed by the interpretation.

PSYCHOANALYTIC THEORY AND THE PHENOMENOLOGICAL ATTITUDE

It is against this background of awareness of the similarities and differences between psychoanalysis and hermeneutics that Ricoeur sets about reading Freud, in order to find what is valuable in psychoanalysis. One valuable aspect of psychoanalysis is its *epistemological* status, by which Ricoeur means its status as a body of knowledge. How *true* are the discoveries, or claims, made by psychoanalysis? To answer this question, it is necessary to realise what kind of science psychoanalysis is. It is what Ricoeur calls a 'historical' science, since it is based on case studies, and a case study is a history of the patient. In fact, it is *because* psychoanalysis is a historical science that it can be a method of interpretation. The natural sciences (chemistry or physics, for example) are *informed* by scientific method, but they are not themselves a method. The method of the natural sciences is inductive – form a hypothesis and then test it through experiment. By this method, the scientist arrives at *the* truth. But 'the problematic of a historical science does not coincide with that of a natural science' (Ricoeur 1970: 374). A historical science does not aim at *the* truth, but at *a* truth that is valid: 'the validity of the interpretations made in psychoanalysis is subject to the same kind of questions as the validity of a historical or exegetical interpretation' (Ricoeur 1970: 374); these are questions along the lines of 'is there a weight of evidence to suggest that this is plausible?' rather than 'can you prove this to be true?' This distinction between the singularity of scientific truth as opposed to the plurality of historical truth is something to which Ricoeur returns when he examines the status of historiography (history writing) in relation to narrative.

Psychoanalysis is, then, like history in that it is not *verifiable*, but instead derives its validity from whether or not it can be shown that what it describes is historically *motivated*. 'Motivated' means that there is a reason that is the probable cause of someone acting in a certain way. But then what differentiates psychoanalysis from history as such? The difference is that the province of history as such is to discover *any* motivation behind behaviour, whereas psychoanalysis is limited to the field whereby the motivation is desire. The 'psychoanalytic point of view on man' is to see man from the perspective of desire, and so 'the function of psychoanalytic theory is to place the work of interpretation within the region of desire' (Ricoeur 1970: 375). The purpose of psychoanalytic *theory* (as opposed to the practice of psychoanalysis) is to set out 'the conditions of possibility of a semantics of desire' (Ricoeur 1970: 375), the conditions whereby it is possible for the meanings that designate desire to be expressed.

What, then, are these conditions? Paradoxically, Ricoeur finds the answer to this question to some extent in phenomenology. Phenomenology puts the body back into Cartesianism, while Descartes himself had taken it out. For the phenomenologist, says Ricoeur (1970: 382), 'a meaning that exists is a meaning caught up within the body, a meaningful behaviour'. Another way of looking at the same thing is to say that 'every praxis [praxis is the putting of an idea into practice] involved in meaning is a signifying or intention made flesh' (Ricoeur 1970: 382); in other words, the body is 'incarnate meaning'. Now, insofar as psychoanalysis is about sexuality, and sexuality is inextricably caught up with the body ('sex in act consists in making us exist as a body, with no distance between us and ourself' (Ricoeur 1970: 382–3)), this insistence by phenomenology that thought cannot be thought other than through the body moves phenomenology 'towards the Freudian unconscious' (Ricoeur 1970: 382).

There is another way in which phenomenology is close to psychoanalysis, and that is in its view of language. The phenomenologist sees language as a way of putting meaning in operation; it is tied in with the body in that just as the body shows that man is capable of behaving, and so is capable of being meaningful (having intentions), so his language is a behaviour which demonstrates what those meanings or intentions are. In making this claim, the phenomenologist is saying something about the *genesis* of language – where it comes from. The psychoanalyst makes a similar claim about the genesis of language. For example, in *Beyond the Pleasure Principle* (1920) Freud tells the story of a small child who plays a simple game whenever his mother is not in the room, of throwing a bobbin on a string away from him and then retrieving it, while uttering the words *fort-da*, 'gone-there'. As Ricoeur (1970: 385) puts it, 'Privation – and consequently presence as well – is signified and transformed into intentionality; being deprived of the mother becomes an intending of the mother.' The little boy overcomes the dialectic of the mother's alternating presence and absence not only by playing the game with the bobbin, but by transforming it into language. It is this transformation which allows him to overcome the trauma of the mother's absence and his overcompensating joy at her return. Overcoming the trauma and the overcompensating joy is the hidden intention behind his discourse, which is expressed through his behaviour becoming a linguistic behaviour. The psychoanalytic and the phenomenological interpretations coincide.

This coincidence leads to another, that of the theory of intersubjectivity. For the phenomenologist, 'the fact that the perceived thing is perceptible by others' (Ricoeur 1970: 386) leads to a reciprocal relation, whereby I recognise others through my recognition that they are recognising me, since to them I must be an object in the field of perception just as they are to me. Psychoanalysis holds the same theory, except that it is expressed through the language of desire. Desire is 'located within an interhuman situation', otherwise 'there would be no such thing as repression, censorship, or wish-fulfilment through fantasies' (Ricoeur 1970: 387). That other people 'are primarily bearers of prohibitions is simply another way of saying that desire encounters another desire – an opposed desire' (Ricoeur 1970: 387). The psychoanalytic 'dialectic' of my relation with other people has the same structure as my phenomenological 'recognition' of other people. Thus phenomenology and psychoanalysis are alike in that they 'are both aiming at the same thing, namely the constitution of the subject, *qua* creature of desire, within an authentic intersubjective discourse' (Ricoeur 1970: 389).

THE *EPOCHÉ* IN REVERSE

And yet, as Ricoeur (1970: 390) says, 'phenomenology is not psychoanalysis'. The difference can, however, only be appreciated at the end of the process (the process of doing phenomenology, or of doing psychoanalysis). This is because 'phenomenology attempts to approach the real history of desire *obliquely*; starting from a perceptual model of consciousness, it gradually generalises that model to embrace all lived or embodied meanings, meanings that are at the same time enacted in the element of language' (Ricoeur 1970: 389–90). Psychoanalysis, meanwhile, 'plunges *directly* into the history of desire', by demanding that the patient simply *tell* the analyst her story. Nevertheless, both psychoanalysis and phenomenology 'have the same aim, the return to true discourse' (Ricoeur 1970: 390).

In his later thinking Freud embarks on what Ricoeur calls an 'antiphenomenology'. This consists in a shift from using the term 'unconscious' as an adjective, to using it as a noun; a shift from using it as an attribute (as in 'unconscious thought processes'), to using it as a substantive (as in '*the* unconscious'). This involves at once a gain in meaning – the unconscious is seen as a system – and a loss of meaning – the term 'unconscious' no longer has a descriptive function. This shift in meaning constitutes what Ricoeur (1970: 118) calls 'an *epochē* in reverse'. The phenomenological *epochē*, or 'reduction', we recall, consists in a bracketing-off of all judgements concerning what we cannot know with certainty – the status of the external world as presented to us through our senses, for example – in order to contemplate what can be known with absolute certainty, namely self-consciousness. The establishment of *the* unconscious is an *epochē* in reverse because 'what is initially best known, the conscious, is suspended and becomes the least known' (Ricoeur 1970: 118). Freud's German term for 'the unconscious' is *das Unbewusste*, 'the unknown'; shortly after turning it into a noun, he renames it *das Es*, 'the it' (which Freud's translators have rendered in Latin as 'the id').

'What we are confronted with', then, in Freud's later thinking, 'is not a reduction *to* consciousness, but a reduction *of* consciousness' (Ricoeur 1970: 424): 'consciousness ceases to be what is best known, and becomes problematic'. In place of the self-evidence of being conscious, there is the process of becoming conscious, as expressed in Freud's (1973: 112) famous formula intended to replace the Cartesian *cogito*, 'Where id was, there Ego shall be.' This constitutes what Ricoeur calls a 'challenge' to the philosophy of reflection. (Phenomenology is a philosophy of reflection, since it is based on the Ego reflecting on itself.) Freud is able to make this intellectual move as a result of the introduction of the concept of 'narcissism' (self-love) into his theory, remembering that in the myth Narcissus falls in love with his own *reflection*. Thus for the Freudian, a philosophy of reflection such as phenomenology, or as expressed in the Cartesian *cogito* ('I think there-fore I am'), is nothing more than an expression of narcissism. It is a philosophical fantasy, an attempt to capture the self to the self, driven by the id which the Ego (that which says 'I' and imagines itself to be the whole person) fails to recognise as a mere expression of self-love, proudly boasting that it has instead discovered some sort of truth.

In his work on narcissism, Freud remarks that psychoanalysis has dealt a third humiliating wound to man. The first was dealt by Copernicus, who realised that man was not the centre of the universe. The second was dealt by Darwin, who realised that man was not at the centre of the animal kingdom. The third and final wound, dealt by Freud, is the realisation that man is not the centre of himself, 'the Ego is not master in his own house'.

Ricoeur (1970: 428) finds Freud's theory of the Ego 'at once very liberating with respect to the illusions of consciousness and very disap-pointing in its inability to give the *I* of the *I think* some sort of meaning'. Ricoeur does not dwell on the way in which psychoanalysis reveals the illusions of consciousness – psychoanalysis is quite capable of doing that for itself. Rather, as a philosopher, Ricoeur is more concerned with the failure of psychoanalysis to lend meaning to the subject, the person who says 'I'. This might seem like an odd claim on Ricoeur's part, since psychoanalysis purports to cure people who are sick, and furthermore to do so through language, as in the 'talking cure'. But this cure lies more in a reconcilement to the alleged fact of life being meaningless, than in a providing of meaning to life. For the psychoanalyst, positing the *cogito*, saying 'I think therefore I am', does not reveal something self-evident (or 'apodictic', as the phenomenologist would say). Rather, being able to say it is the result of the Ego being the product of a *system*: it is an 'economic function' of the Ego to be able to declare 'I think, I am'. In other words, there is a whole system of the psyche at work whereby the various elements within it balance one another through a series of gifts and exchanges; the *cogito* is a gift from the id to the Ego in order to keep it feeling secure. Through this theory, consciousness becomes dispossessed (of the claim to certainty); moreover, through *accepting* psychoanalytic theory, consciousness comes to *realise* that it is dispossessed. 'Realise' here is to be taken literally: the unconscious, or the id, is *made real* by psychoanalytic theory. It is the alleged fact that the unconscious is a real thing, an 'it', that allows the psychoanalyst to claim that it has agency, that it can do things such as deceive us into thinking that the *cogito* is a guarantor of our existence. Ricoeur's (1970: 429) riposte to this is robust: 'considered by itself, . . . this realism is unintelligible; the dispossession of consciousness would be *senseless* if it merely succeeded in distorting reflection into the consideration of a thing'. In other words, if on reflecting on myself in Cartesian or phenomenological style all I found were a thing, an Ego or an id, the thing found would be senseless, since it is only people, not things, who can make language meaningful, imbue it with intention, intention being that which lends an *attitude* towards the language expressed (when I say 'it is raining' I can believe it, whereas a thing such as a computer is incapable of having such an attitude). By insisting on the reality of the id, Freud, says Ricoeur (1970: 439), also ends up insisting on the ideality of meaning. Meaning is not real in psychoanalysis, but ideal, insofar as it is reached at the end of the analysis, 'elaborated in the analytic experience and through the language of transference'. Meaning is not produced by the subject intending something, but is instead lent to the subject from the analyst (this is 'transference') in the experience of undergoing analysis.

This puts the analyst in a very powerful position, as one who not only interprets, but who also provides *the* answer to the problem of meaning. But this would turn psychoanalysis into a claimant for absolute truth, which is inconsistent with its status as a historical, rather than a natural, science. Freud presumes too much. Ricoeur's understanding of psychoanalysis as a hermeneutics, though, rescues psychoanalysis from its (or rather, Freud's) claim to a *universal* explanation for all aspects of the human condition. Psychoanalysis reveals *a* truth about the human condition, the truth of humans' desires, but this is but one of the many truths about humanity, which it is the task of other modes of hermeneutics to reveal. One telling example invoked by Ricoeur is the Oedipus complex.

OEDIPUS

Freud's reading of Sophocles' play *Oedipus Rex* is that Oedipus, in slaying his father and marrying his mother, 'merely shows us the fulfilment of our own childhood wishes', and that the guilt suffered by Oedipus is a manifestation of the repression of those wishes we all undergo in our transformation from amoral children to moral adults. Ricoeur (1970: 516) challenges this reading 'with a second interpretation'. According

OEDIPUS REX

A play written by the Greek tragedian Sophocles (495 BC–405 BC) in c. 426 BC. As an unwanted baby Oedipus is exposed on a hillside, but he unexpectedly survives, unbeknown to his parents. As a young man he has an altercation with a fellow traveller at a crossroads, and kills him. Later in life, Oedipus becomes King of Thebes, and marries a noblewoman, Jocasta. Misfortune befalls the city, and Oedipus curses whoever has brought it. The Theban seer, Tiresias, reveals that it is Oedipus himself who has brought misfortune upon the city, since he has unwittingly killed his father and married his mother. In order to save the city Oedipus must submit to the punishment he has already decreed and become exiled, but meanwhile, in a fit of rage at Jocasta's suicide, he stabs himself in the eyes, blinding himself.

to Ricoeur, 'Sophocles' creation does not aim at reviving the Oedipus complex in the minds of the spectators'; instead, his is a 'tragedy of self-consciousness, of self-recognition'. Oedipus' guilt is not a childlike guilt for having married his mother (after all, he did not *know* it was his mother), but an adult guilt at his own arrogance and anger:

> At the beginning of the play Oedipus calls down curses upon the unknown person responsible for the plague, but he excludes the possibility that that person might in fact be himself. The entire drama consists in the resistance and ultimate collapse of this presumption. Oedipus must be broken in his pride through suffering; this presumption is no longer the culpable desire of the child, but the pride of the king; the tragedy is not the tragedy of Oedipus the child, but of Oedipus Rex.
>
> (Ricoeur 1970: 516)

This is why 'Oedipus becomes guilty precisely because of his pretension to exonerate himself from a crime that, ethically speaking, he is in fact not guilty of' (Ricoeur 1970: 516).

Freud's theory presupposes, against the run of the text, that Oedipus *is* ethically guilty of his crime, which would only be the case had he *known* that Jocasta was his mother. But Oedipus is punished not for marrying Jocasta, but for his presumption, his pride. The evidence in support of this view is to be found in the character of Tiresias the seer:

> The seer . . . is the figure of comedy at the heart of tragedy, a figure Oedipus
> will rejoin only through suffering and pain. The underlying link between
> the anger of Oedipus and the power of truth is thus the core of the veritable
> tragedy. The core is not the problem of sex, but the problem of light. The seer
> is blind with respect to the eyes of his body, but he sees the truth in the light
> of the mind. That is why Oedipus, who sees the light of day but is blind
> with regard to himself, will achieve self-consciousness only by becoming the
> blind seer.

(Ricoeur 1970: 517)

Thus we have two readings: Freud's, which appears antithetical to
the intention of the play, and Ricoeur's, which is antithetical to Freud's.
But Ricoeur does not wish to discount Freud's reading in positing his own. Rather, he 'combine[s] the two readings in the unity of
the symbol in its power to disguise and reveal' (Ricoeur 1970: 517).
Freud's is not a false reading, but an incomplete one. It sees the drama
as a tragedy of origin, rather than as a tragedy of truth. The warning of
the tragedy is, according to Freud, not to let your childhood fantasies
carry over into your adult life, rather than, as in the 'antithetical'
reading, not as an adult to let your anger and pride ('passions', in the
sense discussed in Ricoeur's *Philosophy of the Will*) get the better of
you. But according to Ricoeur, the first, Freudian, reading presupposes
the second reading, or, to put it the other way around, it is impossible
to conceive of the 'antithetical' reading without it being antithetical *of*
the Freudian reading. There is, says Ricoeur, a 'secret alliance' between
the two readings, and this 'resides in the overdetermination of the
symbol itself' (Ricoeur 1970: 519). The symbol is *overdetermined* in that
Oedipus does not only suffer the punishment imposed on him as king,
namely that he is exiled, but he also suffers the punishment he imposes
on himself as a man, namely his blinding. The second punishment is
inflicted in a moment of anger; it is another instance of succumbing to
the passions akin to the first instance when Oedipus imposed the first
punishment in his role as king. Thus although there are two punish-
ments, the second replicates the origin of the first. Tiresias the seer is
the link between the two: the first punishment is motivated by anger
prompted by Tiresias; in the second punishment, Oedipus becomes
just like Tiresias, again in a fit of anger. So, even though the play is
not 'about' the Oedipus complex, as Freud thinks it is, nevertheless
without the overcoming of the Oedipus complex that is symbolised by

there being a second punishment, there could not be an arrival at self-knowledge on Oedipus' part. And so it is with life, which is what gives the play its universal applicability: the Oedipus complex does not explain the whole of life, but nevertheless it is something which must be overcome if we are to proceed in our lives to self-consciousness or self-understanding.

RELIGION

If Ricoeur's re-reading of *Oedipus Rex* shows that Freud provides a partial, rather than complete, truth concerning the human condition, then the same is true of Freud's views on religion. 'For Freud', says Ricoeur (1970: 534), 'religion is the monotonous repetition of its own origins.' It is a manifestation of the return of the repressed, in which each time you try to kill the father (a desire inherited from the Oedipus complex) he returns in a new guise: in Christianity, for example, as Christ, as Moses, or as God – which is why God is called the 'father'. According to Ricoeur (1970: 534), 'Freud's exclusive attention to repetition becomes a refusal to consider a possible epigenesis [a coming into being through matter being built up] of religious feeling, that is to say, a transformation or conversion of desire and fear. This refusal does not seem to me to be based upon analysis, but merely expresses Freud's personal unbelief.' Ricoeur (1970: 534) notices that throughout Freud's works there is a 'paring down' of religious feeling 'when it is about to go beyond the bounds in which it has been confined'. Ricoeur (1970: 540–1) does not deny the importance of repetition in myths: 'ethnology, comparative mythology, biblical exegesis – all confirm that every myth is an interpretation of an earlier account'. He merely denies that the explanation of the myth ends there, or that it can be internalised as 'repression' of the 'Oedipus complex': 'the important factor is not so much this "sensory matter" as the movement of interpretation that is contained in the advancement of meaning and constitutes the intentional forming of the "matter"' (Ricoeur 1970: 541). Put more simply, what is important is not that the myth is repeated, but that each time it is repeated, its meaning is added to and thereby transformed. This transformation means that even if the original myth is a manifestation of the childhood desire to kill the father, this is no longer true of the subsequent versions. To return to a point made in Ricoeur's earlier *Symbolism of Evil*, a myth already interprets its own roots. The

Christ story is not so much a repetition of the Moses story, but a reinterpretation of it.

Myths – particularly religious myths – have, then, as well as an *archeological* meaning, a *teleological* one: their meaning is not only of the origin of man, but also of where he is going. Again, myths, like works of art such as tragedies, are not about the child but about the adult, although again what makes them pertinent to life is that, as in life, the adult contains the child within it. Freud remains at the stage of the archeological, and does not proceed to the teleological. But to understand myths, or the symbols of the sacred, one cannot simply deny the Freudian reading. The Freudian reading is not sufficient in itself, but is a necessary part of the whole picture:

> If symbols are fantasies that have been denied and overcome, they are never fantasies that have been abolished. That is why one is never certain that a given symbol of the sacred is not simply a 'return of the repressed'; or rather, it is always certain that each symbol of the sacred is also and at the same time a revival of an infantile and archaic symbol. The two functions of symbol remain inseparable. The symbolic meanings closest to theological and philosophical speculation are always involved with some trace of an archaic myth. This close alliance of archaism and prophecy constitutes the richness of religious symbolism; it also constitutes its ambiguity.
>
> (Ricoeur 1970: 543)

This ambiguity means that for the believer, having read Freud, belief can never be the same again. The religious believer must recognise the desire behind religion, which is for consolation. But recognition that the believer desires consolation does not invalidate belief. Psychoanalysis can also learn something from religion, or at least from religious philosophy, and that is concerning the nature of reality: 'reality is not simply a set of observable facts and verifiable laws; reality is also, in psychoanalytic terms, the world of things and of men' (Ricoeur 1970: 550). If this is so, then psychoanalysis should not consign myths, fables and stories to the realm of the unreal, false and illusory, as Freud seeks to do when he explains them as manifestations of a denial of the truth behind existence, the alleged truth of the Oedipus complex. Myths do not deny the truth, but tell it: they are 'the symbolic exploration of our relationship to beings and to Being' (Ricoeur 1970: 551). In this way, they not only teach us that we must submit to necessity (the necessity of our being born, as the psychoanalyst would have it), but also that we are capable of loving creation. Reality is not a mere necessity to be submitted to; it is also a creation to be loved.

SUMMARY

Despite the apparent differences between the two disciplines, Ricoeur sets out to demonstrate that psychoanalysis is a hermeneutics. It is a hermeneutics of desire; Freud's failing is in not realising that although psychoanalysis is an adequate explanation of 'the semantics of desire', that is the limit of its field of enquiry. Psychoanalysis is a historical, rather than a natural, science: it does not aim at verifiable truths, but at plausible explanations. Psychoanalysis is also a phenomenological *epochē*, or reduction, in reverse, in that what in phenomenology is held to be the most known, consciousness, becomes the least known. Reflective philosophy, as expressed in the Cartesian 'I think therefore I am', is for the psychoanalyst merely an expression of narcissism. But if this were wholly the case, the psychoanalyst would be a repository of the kind of absolute truth that would be inconsistent with psychoanalysis being a historical, rather than a natural, science. That psychoanalysis grasps the truth about desire, but that the truth of desire is not the whole truth of human existence, is shown in Freud's interpretations of art and religion. The tragedy of Oedipus does not merely demonstrate the 'Oedipus complex', but also shows the consequences of anger and presumption; it can only show one of these aspects of the human condition by showing the other. Religious myths, meanwhile, do not merely repeat themselves, and so are not merely manifestations of repression. They also reinterpret themselves, and in so doing demonstrate that reality is not merely a necessity to be submitted to, but is also a creation to be loved.

4

METAPHOR

Subsequent to writing *The Symbolism of Evil* Ricoeur came to see that interpreting symbols alone was not sufficient for hermeneutics. *The Symbolism of Evil* had separated out myths and their symbolic status from the language in which they were expressed, assuming the language itself to be perfectly transparent. But of course, the problem of double meaning can occur at the linguistic level as well. By the late 1960s, when Ricoeur has extended hermeneutics from being a theory of interpretation to a theory of interpretation through *reading*, the problem of meaning at the linguistic level becomes something he needs to address. This he does entirely within one substantial self-contained work, *La métaphore vive* (1975; *The Rule of Metaphor*, 1977).

The Rule of Metaphor consists of eight studies, which together constitute a progressive examination of metaphor within three entities: the word, the sentence and discourse. According to Ricoeur, metaphor at the level of the word is the domain of rhetoric; metaphor at the level of the sentence is the domain of semantics; and metaphor at the level of discourse is the domain of hermeneutics. Finally, the eighth study elucidates 'the philosophy implicit in the theory of metaphorical reference' (Ricoeur 1977: 7). As Ricoeur (1977: 7) explains, however, the book

does not seek to replace rhetoric with semantics and the latter with hermeneutics, and thus have one refute the other, but rather seeks to justify each approach within the limits of the corresponding discipline and to demonstrate the systematic continuity of viewpoints by following the progression from word to sentence and from sentence to discourse.

As is Ricoeur's manner, the book is patient, in that it not only posits its own theory of metaphor, but engages in a thorough explanation and critique of the other theories that have been posited since Aristotle, being almost encyclopaedic in its coverage of the topic.

METAPHOR, MIMESIS AND ACTION

Ricoeur begins his exploration of metaphor with a critique of Aristotle's theory. For Ricoeur, the most important part of the theory is the 'seeing-as' aspect of metaphor: metaphor allows us to see a familiar thing in a new light. In another of his works, the *Poetics*, composed at about the same time as the *Rhetoric*, Aristotle discusses *mimesis*. 'Mimesis' means 'imitation', and Plato had used the term very broadly to mean anything resembling anything else in any sort of way. In particular, Plato thought nature itself to be *mimetic* of an ideal world, so that a painting of nature would be an imitation of an imitation. Rejecting Platonic philosophy, Aristotle gives a much stricter, narrower definition of mimesis. For him, mimesis must involve *making*: it is the specifically human activity of creating one thing to be like another thing. Mimesis is not the mere imitation, accidental or otherwise, of something, but the deliberate creation of something in order to represent something else. In other words, as Ricoeur points out, there is a direct parallel between mimesis (as described in Aristotle's *Poetics*) and metaphor (as described in his *Rhetoric*): metaphor is to simile what mimesis is to imitation.

For Aristotle, then, mimesis is not an imitation, but a representation. The difference is crucial, insofar as imitation *per se* is concerned with appearance, whereas mimesis is the *imitation of an action*. In other words, mimesis involves plot (*muthos*). *Muthos* 'is not just a rearrangement of human action into a more coherent form, but a structuring that elevates the action'; it is therefore through *muthos* that mimesis 'preserves and represents that which is human, not just in its essential features, but in a way that makes it greater and nobler' (Ricoeur 1977: 40). Now, Ricoeur wants to 'apply a still more closely fitting relationship' between Aristotle's theory of mimesis and his theory of metaphor.

ARISTOTLE (384–22 BC)

Along with Plato the most significant of the ancient Greek philosophers, Aristotle is generally credited with being the first to divide philosophy into its disciplines, such as ethics, legal philosophy, political philosophy etc. His most important distinction was between *physics* – the stuff of material nature – and *metaphysics*, that which lies beyond the natural world, and is therefore the province of purely intellectual enquiry. Aristotle's overriding interest was in the problem of how we can proceed from what we know by observation, to what is known by nature, which we must discover through the operation of the intellect. Along the route of this enquiry, he invented *logical* thinking, and most importantly the *syllogism* ('if all A is B and all B is C, then all A is C').

In his *Rhetoric*, Aristotle locates metaphoricity at the level of the word (*lexis*), and posits for it three defining features: metaphor is something that happens to the noun, metaphor is defined in terms of movement (*epiphora*), and metaphor is the transposition of a name. Aristotle's own example is 'Achilles is a lion'. Here we see that the metaphor hinges on the two nouns, 'Achilles' and 'lion', and that the name 'Achilles' is transposed or shifted (this is the *epiphora*) onto the lion. What this comes down to is the idea of *substitution* – one word for another, and one thing for another, the words being thing-words (nouns). But not any substitution will do – the effect must be *allotrios*, alien, insofar as the transposition should be from ordinary, current or usual terminology to unusual usage – otherwise there would be no point in the metaphor. Metaphor, then, borrows from one domain (in this case, that of animals), and is a substitution for a word belonging to another domain (of people). Thus metaphor says what is not proper – Achilles is not a lion, he is a person – but this is allowable ('poetic licence') so long as the rules of the relationship between the terms are understood. In this case, the relationship is one of equality – we can say that Achilles is a lion because he is *like* a lion – but other relationships can pertain, such as genus to species or species to genus.

For Aristotle, although metaphor is akin to simile (saying something is *like* something), it is also superior to simile, insofar as it is shorter and thus conveys new knowledge in a more succinct way. And herein lies the importance of metaphor for Aristotle: because metaphor borrows its terms from unexpected sources, it surprises and delights the reader along with providing new information, and so the knowledge conveyed is impressed upon the reader the more forcibly. 'Achilles is like a lion' is merely a piece of more or less interesting information, but 'Achilles *is* a lion' places things before our eyes, says Aristotle, makes us see things.

According to Aristotle in the *Rhetoric*, the strange and noble meet in the good metaphor. According to Aristotle in the *Poetics*, meanwhile, mimesis is elevated to the noble as a result of *muthos*. Ricoeur's original contribution, which 'goes beyond Aristotle's intentions', is

> to ask whether the secret of metaphor, as a displacement of meaning at the level of words, does not rest in the elevation of meaning at the level of *muthos*. And if this proposal is acceptable, then metaphor would not only be a deviation in relation to ordinary usage, but also, by means of this deviation, the privileged instrument in that upward motion of meaning promoted by *mimesis*.
>
> (Ricoeur 1977: 41)

In other words, for Ricoeur metaphor is important because it is the instrument by which mimesis, imitation, becomes *muthos*, plot, and therefore not merely an imitation of nature, but an imitation of human action. We want to see the imitation of a human action, in a tragedy, say, because that imitation is elevated – it shows the nobility of humanity, and so is uplifting. Metaphoric language, as a deviation from the norm, is also elevated language, and so the language proper to poetic composition is metaphorical language.

So far this might appear as a theory of metaphor merely of interest in its slight embellishment of Aristotle's theory. But Ricoeur wants to make a grander philosophical claim. The point of his lengthy analysis of Aristotle is to remind us 'that no discourse ever suspends our belonging to the world' (Ricoeur 1977: 43): 'through mimesis metaphor's deviations from normal lexis belong to the great enterprise of "saying what is"'. Moreover, this 'saying what is' is not just a saying of how things are in nature, but – because of its role in *muthos*, plot – metaphor allows mimesis to 'serve as an *index* for that dimension of reality that does not receive due account in the simple description of that-thing-over-there' (Ricoeur 1977: 43). Metaphorical discourse presents all things not only as being, but as acting – all being has a potential for acting, and this potential 'blossoms forth' in metaphorical language. As Ricoeur (1977: 43) pithily summarises, '*Lively* expression is that which expresses existence as alive.' Consider, for example, the proposition 'Faith will enable us to derive some hope from our despair.' This is hardly likely to rouse the addressees of this utterance to action. But now consider the same ideas expressed in the words of Martin Luther King Jr (King 1963): 'With this faith we will be able to hew out of the mountain of despair a stone of hope.' Through metaphor abstract language here is made concrete, and consequently it becomes the language of action.

METAPHOR AS A TROPE

We can already see how Ricoeur is moving from analysis of lexis (the word) to analysis of the sentence, or, in his terms, from rhetoric to semantics. He completes this movement by engaging in *tropology*, the analysis of tropes.

> ### TROPE
>
> A figure of speech whereby a word or phrase is used in a sense other than its normal or usual one; a verbal embellishment of language.

According to Ricoeur, tropology traditionally depends upon the notion of the 'semantic *lacuna*'. A lacuna is a gap in meaning; a semantic lacuna is a gap in a sentence that the author wishes to fill. The gap is filled with an improper, or deviant, word, which is borrowed from a different sphere of discourse – it is an alien term. The borrowed alien term is substituted for the absent term in the sentence either as a matter of preference on the part of the author, which constitutes a trope proper, or because there is a gap in the author's vocabulary, which constitutes *catachresis*.

> ### CATACHRESIS
>
> 'Improper use of words; application of a term to a thing which it does not properly denote; abuse or perversion of a trope or metaphor' (*Oxford English Dictionary*).

Whichever, there is a relationship between the figurative sense of the borrowed word and the proper meaning of the absent word, and this is the 'reason' (rationale or basis) behind the substitution of terms. There are several different 'reasons' behind the substitution of terms, each constituting a *figure of speech* that can be named and categorised: if the 'reason' is *resemblance*, for example, then the figure of speech is a metaphor. According to the traditional or classical theory, 'to explain (or understand) a trope is to be guided by the trope's "reason" . . . in finding the absent proper word: thus, it is to restore the proper term for which an improper term had been substituted' (Ricoeur 1977: 46). Since each trope hinges on one term, to restore the 'original', proper term in the place of the substituted, figurative term is to understand the trope completely or *exhaustively*.

Ricoeur then turns to the last exponent of the classical theory of tropes, the nineteenth-century French grammarian Pierre Fontanier, who in his *Figures of Discourse* (1830) attempted a systematic categorisation of all of the tropes of rhetoric. For Fontanier, the meaning of the trope rests on the relation between the idea signified by the substituted figurative word, and the idea signified by the absent proper word – it is this which constitutes the trope's 'reason'. Fontanier identifies three species of such relations. First, relations of *correlation* constitute metonymy, as in 'Shall we have another bottle?', where 'bottle' refers to its contents. Second, relations of *connection* constitute synecdoche, as in 'I see a sail!', where 'sail' refers to the ship of which it is a part. And third, relations by *resemblance* constitute metaphor, as in 'Go for it, tiger!', where 'tiger' refers to the person addressed. Examples of relations of correlation are 'cause to effect, instrument to purpose, container to content, thing to its location, sign to signification, physical to moral, model to thing' (Ricoeur 1977: 56) – in each of these cases, the two objects are brought together, but each constitutes a separate whole, entailing the concept of 'excluded from'. Relations of connection, meanwhile, entail the concept of 'included in', as in the case of 'relations of part to whole, of material to thing, of one to many, of species to genus, of abstract to concrete, of species to individual' (Ricoeur 1977: 56). There is a perfect symmetry between metonymy and synecdoche: in both cases, one idea is designated by the name of another, and then the relationship is either one of '. . . is excluded from . . .', or one of '. . . is included in . . .'.

What makes Fontanier's account interesting for Ricoeur is that metaphor does not belong to this symmetrical pair. For one thing, metaphor can be attached to any kind of word, whereas the other tropes can only attach to nouns. As with his treatment of Aristotle, Ricoeur is here prepared to go beyond Fontanier's intentions. Fontanier wanted to keep the discussion of tropes at the level of individual words, rather than assign them to propositions, not least because he adhered to the eighteenth-century belief that words were the designation of thoughts, and that propositions were merely the combination of thoughts expressed through the combination of words. But Ricoeur sees in Fontanier's theory of metaphor an unwitting shift from the word to the proposition. Even in the metaphorical use of a noun, as described by Fontanier ('to make a tiger of an angry man', or 'to make of a great writer a swan'), there is already something other than merely designating a thing by a new name. 'Is it not', asks Ricoeur (1977: 57), '"naming" in the sense of characterising, of qualifying?' It is for this reason – that the substitution of resemblance involves an *attribution* – that metaphor can attach to words other than nouns, as in Fontanier's other examples such as '*consuming* remorse', 'courage *craving* for peril and praise', or 'his *seething* spirit'. As Ricoeur (1977: 57) points out, 'these metaphors do not name' (as Fontanier claims they do), 'but characterise what has already been named'. Moreover, in order to do this they must not only involve individual words, but the whole sentence which contains them. This is 'because they function only within a sentence that relates not just two ideas but also two words, namely one term taken non-metaphorically, which acts as a support, and the other taken metaphorically, which fulfils the function of characterisation' (Ricoeur 1977: 57).

The important point about this for Ricoeur is that, contrary to Fontanier's own conclusion, metaphor points towards propositions, and is not confined to the level of the individual word. Fontanier is blinded to the consequences of his own theory. This blindness, for example, prevents him from seeing allegory as an extended metaphor, whereas for Ricoeur allegory is metaphor operating explicitly at the level of the proposition. In fact, once metaphor is, so to speak, liberated from the word, then all description can be seen as metaphorical insofar as it sets an object before our eyes in a certain way – description is not so much *seeing* as *seeing as*.

'Seeing as' is, for Ricoeur, what figurative language consists of. Fontanier is valuable in distinguishing metaphor from metonymy and synecdoche: in Ricoeur's terms, of the three only metaphor consists of 'seeing as', or properly figurative language. And what, in turn, is important about figurative language is that it is 'free', in that any idea can be freely presented under the image of another. Any piece of language can be metaphorical of anything – that is the freedom that figurative language opens up. In turn, it follows that a 'good' metaphor is a newly invented one. As Fontanier himself acknowledges, old meta-phors tend to look like ordinary language (people forget that they *are* metaphors), whereas new metaphors entail the exercise of freedom in language. In this sense, freedom in language is for Ricoeur a marker of human inventiveness.

METAPHOR AND SEMANTICS

Ricoeur's next move is away from an analysis of the word, to an analysis of the sentence and then of discourse. This is not to say that the lexical analyses of Aristotle and Fontanier were *wrong*, but merely that they either became restricted to *classifying* metaphor rather than *describing* how it produces meaning, or, when they try to describe meaning, they inevitably go beyond the word alone, despite their claims to the con-trary. Ricoeur, meanwhile, is interested in the *sentence* as a unit of mean-ing, because it is a whole not reducible to the sum of its parts. In order to arrive at his own view of the metaphoricity of sentences, Ricoeur turns to the theories of four twentieth-century writers: the British literary theorist I. A. Richards (1893–1979), the Azerbaijani-American émigré philosopher Max Black (1909–88), the American aestheti-cian Monroe Beardsley (1915–85) and the Russian-American émigré linguist Roman Jakobson (1896–1982).

I. A. RICHARDS

In his *The Philosophy of Rhetoric* (1936), Richards (1936: 3) calls rhetoric 'a study of misunderstanding and its remedies', and attacks what he calls the 'Proper Meaning Superstition'. For Richards words have no 'proper' meanings; no meaning can be said to 'belong' to them: words do not possess any meaning in themselves, because it is discourse, taken as an undivided whole, that carries the meaning. Richards' is unashamedly a *contextual* theory: the meaning of a word has to be 'guessed' by a reader or listener each time the word appears, according to the context in which it is being used. Dictionary definitions only provide a rough guide as to the area of meaning occupied by a word; they do not anchor the word in a once-and-for-all stabilised meaning. Meaning comes from the interplay of words with one another in the context of discourse, not from dictionaries. Meaning is ever invented anew.

When it comes to metaphor, this theory leads Richards directly to the contrary position from that of Aristotle. For Richards, language is 'vitally metaphorical'; metaphor is the very stuff of ordinary usage, and is not something that needs to be taught as a deviation from such usage. Metaphor holds together within one simple meaning two different parts of different contexts of the word's possible meanings. It is no longer a case, as with Aristotle and Fontanier, of a proper meaning and a deviation from it into a figurative meaning; rather, metaphor is 'a transaction between contexts', neither of which have privileged or underprivileged status as 'proper' or 'deviant'.

Richards calls the underlying idea the *tenor*, and the idea through which the underlying idea is arrived at the *vehicle*. Thus, to use the example of 'Achilles is a lion', the tenor (underlying idea) is the strength, courage and nobility of Achilles, and the vehicle is the idea of a lion. But thinking of a lion does not of itself bring to mind Achilles: only on reading the sentence as a whole that makes this proposal is this achieved. Therefore, the metaphor is not the tenor or the vehicle alone, but the sum of both. Moreover, the choice of vehicle *alters* the tenor: now, Achilles will forever not only be thought of as strong, courageous and noble (he was thought of in those terms before the metaphor was coined), but also as 'lionlike', which is something else over and above strength, courage and nobility, although it encompasses those attributes.

As is his practice, Ricoeur accepts Richards' theory up to a point, before adapting it to his own ends. His first criticism of the theory is that it does not distinguish between literal and metaphorical meaning: if the sole criterion of metaphor is that it presents two meanings at once, well, literal meaning can do that too (a model of Humpty Dumpty made from lard is *fat*). Moreover, the theory does not distinguish between cases where there is a *resemblance* between tenor and vehicle (Humpty Dumpty and an egg), and cases where there is a *shared characteristic* between them (Achilles and the lion). And finally, the theory does not address what Ricoeur calls the 'ontological' status of metaphor – its relation to how things actually are. This is a problem of the relationship between belief, understanding and truth. As Ricoeur (1977: 83) asks, 'Must we believe what an utterance says in order to understand it fully? Must we accept as true what the Bible or the *Divine Comedy* says metaphorically?'

MAX BLACK

In his *Models and Metaphors* (1962), Black begins by defining metaphor as simultaneously being dependent on a whole sentence, and hinging on one word: metaphor is 'a sentence or another expression in which *some* words are used metaphorically while the remainder are used non-metaphorically' (Black 1962: 27), as in 'The chairman ploughed through the discussion', in which the word *ploughed* is taken metaphorically, and the others not. Instead of Richards' *tenor* and *vehicle*, Black favours the more precise terms *focus* and *frame* to name the metaphorical word in a sentence and the rest of the sentence respectively. But like Richards, Black recognises that the metaphor as a whole is dependent on the *interaction* between the two parts, focus and frame.

This more precise definition of metaphor allows Black to consider *how* metaphors work in giving rise to new meaning. The example given to explain this is 'Man is a wolf.' According to Black, the focus, 'wolf', operates not according to its current meaning. If we look up the word 'wolf' in a dictionary we might find something along the lines of 'carnivorous wild animal, allied to dog', but this is not what we primarily think of in understanding the metaphor. Rather, a 'system of associated commonplaces' comes into play, and these vary according to the various predispositions of the reader depending on of which community of speakers he or she is a member. When speaking of a particular person as a wolf, a whole array of commonplaces is brought to mind which, says Black, *organises* our view of the person, so that the metaphor acts as a screen or filter through which the person is seen: metaphor confers 'insight'. In this way, metaphor cannot be explained exhaustively in the way Fontanier, for example, claimed it could be.

Ricoeur's (1977: 88) judgement on Black's theory is that it has 'great merits', but nevertheless he has 'some reservations'. Ricoeur's primary objection is that the theory only works with established connotations – we all (in the English-speaking world) *already* know what wolf-like features are. But the really interesting connotations for Ricoeur are those that are created anew, for example in literature. Moreover, Black's theory does not take into account that once the metaphor 'man is a wolf' is established, not only do we never see man in the same way again, but also we never see wolves in the same way again, either: 'the wolf appears more human at the same moment that by calling a man a wolf one places the man in a special light' (Ricoeur

1977: 88). Ricoeur still wants to know *where* this additional meaning comes from.

MONROE BEARDSLEY

In his *Aesthetics* (1958) and the article 'The Metaphorical Twist' (1962), Beardsley sees metaphor as being part of the general strategy of literary composition. This strategy is one of *meaning* something incompatible with, or even the opposite of, what is *stated*. Thus oxymoron – *living death* – for example, is part of the same strategy, as is irony, when the writer suggests the contrary of what he's saying by withdrawing his statement at the very point of making it. In metaphor, contradiction or 'logical absurdity', is not as direct as in these cases, but is still present. For example, if streets are described as 'metaphysical', the reader is invited to draw connotations from the word *metaphysical*, despite the manifestly physical nature of streets. According to Beardsley, a *metaphor* is any such case of indirect self-contradiction.

Ricoeur finds two advantages in Beardsley's theory of metaphor. First, we can redefine 'proper' and 'figurative' meaning. 'Proper meaning' can now be called the dictionary meaning of a term. But 'figurative meaning' is no longer a *deviant* meaning of a particular word; instead, it is the meaning of the whole statement that arises from giving a particular subject a self-contradictory attribute. A better term would be 'emergent meaning', since this kind of meaning only has existence in the here and now of the particular sentence in which it is being used. Second, Beardsley's theory works in relation to newly invented metaphor, in a way Black's does not, and this allows Ricoeur (1977: 97) to claim that 'metaphorical attribution is superior to every other use of language in showing what "living speech" really is'.

The main point of Ricoeur's detour through the theories of Richards, Black and Beardsley is to promote a view of man's relation to language which is optimistic, in that it sees language as a liberating force which expands the horizon of human well-being, rather than being a 'prison house' as some have claimed it to be. Language is alive and a force for life. Literature becomes the vehicle for this human attainment, and thus the pinnacle of human achievement:

> A significant trait of living language is the power always to push the frontier of non-sense further back. There are probably no words so incompatible that

some poet could not build a bridge between them; the power to create new contextual meanings seems to be truly limitless. Attributions that appear to be 'non-sensical' can make sense in some unexpected context. No speaker ever completely exhausts the connotative possibilities of words.

(Ricoeur 1977: 95)

ROMAN JAKOBSON

The final phase of Ricoeur's discussion of metaphor at the level of the sentence consists of a critique of the work of Roman Jakobson. Jakobson's major contribution to the study of metaphor arises out of his discussion of linguistic aspects of *aphasia* (loss of speech as a result of brain damage). Jakobson's is a *binary* theory, derived from the view that all production of language involves two processes on the part of the speaker: combination and selection. At any point in his discourse, a speaker must at once *select* a word from his word stock, and also *combine* that word with other words to create meaning. The process of combining words manifests itself in *association* (one word being placed next to another), and this Jakobson calls the *metonymic* pole of language. An example of a metonymy is *Washington* in 'Washington condemned Iraqi aggression', where *Washington* means 'the US Government'. We know it means this, because Washington is *already associated* with the US Government (it is the place where the Government is based). The process of selecting words, meanwhile, manifests itself in *similarity* (one word meaning something *like* another), and Jakobson calls this the *metaphoric* pole of language. An example of a metaphor is *table* in 'Fred Bloggs is a table.' From this it is not readily apparent why Fred Bloggs is a table, until it is explained that Fred is a square, and has a wooden personality. Thus the metaphor *creates* the link between term and whatever it is being compared to, whereas in metonymy the link is already there. Jakobson's theory reduces *all* figurative language to one or other of these two poles, metaphor or metonymy (and ultimately the theory claims that all language whatever is orientated towards one or other of these poles). Thus, for example, simile is a subdivision of metaphor, and synecdoche (part for whole) is a subdivision of metonymy.

According to Ricoeur (1977: 178), 'the strength of Jakobson's schema is also its weakness'. The strength is that it is applicable to all language, and is very simple. But the theory has the same weaknesses as all the other theories that based metaphor on the single word in isolation, and not on the whole sentence. Paradoxically, it is because the one distinction that Jakobson makes is between metaphor and metonymy that the distinction between metaphor and metonymy becomes blurred. After all, metonymy is itself a species of substitution – *knife* for *fork*, say – and so substitution cannot be the defining characteristic of metaphor. If the only difference between metaphor and metonymy lies in the *kind* of substitution, then this becomes a purely subjective criterion, since someone might not know that *knife* is already associated with *fork*, and so for that person the substitution would be metaphorical and not metonymic. Conversely, Jakobson's theory again fails to distinguish between metaphors in common use and newly coined metaphors. A metaphor in common use looks a bit like a metonymy according to Jakobson's definition, since the link between the two terms (the 'original' term and the substituted term) is as familiar as the knowledge that Washington is the seat of the US Government. So, we are once again back with Ricoeur's hostility towards *substitution of terms* as being what defines metaphor, and his opposition to treating metaphor as hinging on single words.

METAPHOR AND HERMENEUTICS

The hostile analysis of metaphor as substitution of individual word one for another, and Ricoeur's critique of those who hold this view, leads him to the position that what is important about metaphor is not the 'semantic clash', or juxtaposition of two meanings (the literal and the figurative) itself, but 'the solution to the enigma' that it presents the listener or reader (Ricoeur 1977: 214). Metaphors are only valuable because they force the listener or reader to interpret them. This work of interpretation – *hermeneutics* again – is itself an intrinsic part of the metaphoric process. As a process, it involves the linking of the word to the context of the whole sentence in which it is located, but also in the cultural context of the discourse in which the sentence is located. This is what it means to be alive – to be an interpreting being – and so it is the metaphorical dimension of language that is most alive in language. Metaphor is that part of language which invites us to do hermeneutics. For this reason Ricoeur is not so much interested in *dead* metaphors, as in *living* ones, and particularly in newly coined metaphors. It is these metaphors that force us to do the work of thinking, because they present a new idea in a new way. It is the primary function of language to provide new knowledge; metaphoric language – so long as 'metaphoric' is correctly defined – also provides new knowledge, but in a way that makes us arrive at it through the work of interpretation. This is the more valuable, because the work of interpretation involved in understanding a metaphor is itself a part of the knowledge arrived at. Metaphor is thus a point in language at which the objective facts of the world meet the subjective interpretation of the individual who interprets them – a point at which *phenomenological truth* is arrived.

Ricoeur understands this phenomenological truth as being reached through a process of 'seeing as'. 'Seeing as' is a notion Ricoeur borrows from *Gestalt* psychology. It is not the same as mere seeing. Mere seeing is simply an experience. But *seeing as* is half way between an experience and an act, or, 'it is an experience and an act at one and the same time' (Ricoeur 1977: 213). So long as one is not blind, one sees. But one either *sees as*, or one does not. It is like those 'magic eye' pictures, which ostensibly consist merely of bands of coloured dots, but when seen in a certain way, reveal a picture. You cannot be *taught* to see a magic eye picture – you either see it or you don't – and some people never do. Metaphor, for Ricoeur, is rather like a linguistic version of a magic eye picture. What is needed in order to understand it is not instruction, but intuition and imagination. Poetic language is the richest kind of language in this respect.

What, then, is poetic language? It is not necessarily the language of poetry, although it is usually found there, as well as in other created works of literature. Ricoeur says that it is language that produces a *heuristic fiction*, in other words, a fiction that leads you to find out, or discover, something. The poetic function of language seeks to re-describe reality by a roundabout route. Metaphor is the vehicle by means of which the route to describing reality is made indirect. When language, through metaphor, 'divests itself of its function of direct description' (Ricoeur 1977: 247), it attains a mythic level where its

GESTALT PSYCHOLOGY

A school of psychology that holds that human perceptions, reactions etc. are *Gestalts*, i.e. structures, forms or configurations which are indivisible wholes. These wholes cannot adequately be described by analysing them in terms of the sums of their parts.

function of discovery is set free. Poetic language, then, has not a descriptive function, but a *redescriptive* function. Metaphorical *truth* is the intention behind this redescription to say something real about the world.

Metaphorical truth is produced by three tensions, and discovering what they are reveals why Ricoeur has taken such a long detour through everyone else's theories before getting to his point. The first tension is within the statement, between (in Richards' terminology) 'tenor' and 'vehicle', or (in Black's terminology) between 'focus' and 'frame'. The second tension is between two interpretations, the literal interpretation and the metaphoric. The third tension is in 'the relational function of the copula', in other words, in the role of the word *is* and how it serves to relate one term to another, as in, for example, 'Achilles is a lion.' On this *is* hinges an interplay of sameness and difference: Achilles is at once the same as a lion, but not a lion. This third tension is the most important of them all for Ricoeur in producing, and defining, metaphorical truth. A metaphor 'preserves the "is not" within the "is"' (Ricoeur 1977: 249). Arriving at metaphorical truth is not a question of judgement on the reader's part. If it were, we would either have to choose between Achilles being a lion or his not being a lion, which would take away the point of the metaphor, or we would have to accept a contradiction (Achilles both is and is not a lion), which would be silly. Rather, arriving at metaphorical truth is a question of the reader suspending, or bracketing off, their judgement regarding the literal truth of the proposition. Understanding metaphor is a phenomenology of reading.

METAPHOR AND PHILOSOPHY

But Ricoeur is not satisfied to end his investigation at this point. As we have seen, Ricoeur is more interested in living metaphor than in dead metaphor (the original French title of his book is *La métaphore vive*, 'metaphor lives' or 'living metaphor'). The final chapter of the book is devoted to 'metaphor and philosophical discourse', and is an attack on a certain strand of philosophy that sees all language as dead metaphor. This notion has its origins in the ideas of the nineteenth-century German philosopher Friedrich Nietzsche (1844–1900), who claimed that 'truths are illusions which we have forgotten are illusions; they are metaphors that have become worn out and have been drained of sensuous force, coins which lost their embossing and are now considered as metal and no longer as coins' (Nietzsche 1979: 84).

Of course, this argument by Nietzsche is itself expressed in metaphorical terms, and this is a theme taken up in a celebrated essay, 'White Mythology' (1971), by Ricoeur's younger contemporary, the French philosopher Jacques Derrida (b. 1930). Derrida's claim is that all philosophising is infected with a blindness to the metaphoricity of the language in which it is expressed. Metaphor is more than a special effect within language; it is the very essence of language. Even a philosophy of metaphor is itself inescapably metaphorical, so that metaphor cannot be adequately defined outside its own system. Metaphor thus runs out of control through language and through philosophy, the whole of philosophical discourse being an edifice built entirely upon itself without grounding in reality, and sustaining itself by an active forgetting of this fact.

Ricoeur calls Nietzsche and Derrida 'philosophers of suspicion': they suspect that there is something wrong with metaphysics, that it is a con, and that its inherent tendency to hoodwink the unwary needs to be exposed. But Ricoeur himself, on the contrary, is not suspicious of metaphysics, and he has faith in its ability to reveal the truth. This is also a faith in the ability of metaphor to tell truth. Ricoeur's central objection to both Nietzsche and Derrida is that their theories only consider dead metaphor (metaphor that its users have forgotten is metaphorical, such as 'toe the line'). Once living metaphor – and, more precisely, the ability to coin new metaphor – is admitted, argues Ricoeur, then the ability of language to increase the store of human knowledge is restored, and the suspicion one might feel towards metaphysics melts away. After all, it is impossible to coin a metaphor without being aware that that is what one is doing, and likewise a new metaphor forces a reader to think it through, and in so doing again be aware of the metaphorical nature of the language she is interpreting.

Indeed, for Ricoeur *living* metaphor is the most significant and noticeable kind of metaphor within language; dead metaphor is a relatively trivial affair, even if it is true that most words within any given language can be shown to be metaphorical derivations of lost originals. Metaphor 'forces conceptual thought to *think more*' (Ricoeur 1977: 303). This is what it has in common with imagination, of which it is the product:

> Metaphor is living not only to the extent that it vivifies a constituted language. Metaphor is living by virtue of the fact that it introduces the spark of

imagination into a 'thinking more' at the conceptual level. This struggle to 'think more', guided by the 'vivifying principle', is the 'soul' of interpretation.

(Ricoeur 1977: 303)

SUMMARY

For Ricoeur, metaphor works not at the level of individual words, but at the level of the sentence. It works not by substituting one 'deviant' term for another 'proper' term, but by the interaction between the 'focus' ('a lion', say) and the 'frame' ('Achilles') within the context of the whole sentence ('Achilles is a lion.'). This entails three tensions: between the focus and the frame, between the literal and the metaphoric meanings, and within the word 'is', which in metaphor also contains the meaning 'is not'. This last tension is important because it is the route to metaphorical truth, which is a way of seeing something *as* something. This seeing something in a certain way sheds new light on the world, and so increases human knowledge. But it only does so as a result of a hermeneutic process on the part of the reader of the metaphor. Metaphor is that part of language that invites interpretation, and thus invites us to do hermeneutics. (For that reason, poetic language, being the most metaphorical, is the language closest to human truth, which is phenomenological truth – the place where the objective truth of the external world and the subjective truth of the reader meet.) We should therefore not be alarmed if certain philosophers show all language to be inherently metaphorical, since such an insight depends on the kind of metaphors involved being dead ones, whereas Ricoeur's is a philosophy of *living* metaphor: it is the creation of new metaphor which not only keeps language alive, but which vivifies human thought through its compulsion to exercise the imagination in an interpretative manner.

5

NARRATIVE

Ricoeur's work on narrative is designed to form a complementary pair with his work on metaphor. For Ricoeur, the attractive aspect of both metaphor and narrative is 'productive invention'. In order to produce a metaphor we must overcome the resistance of our current categorisations of language by a process of what Ricoeur calls 'predicative assimilation': in other words, we say something *is* something else, and in so doing assimilate the something else into the first something, despite the fact that on first appearance it does not belong there. This constitutes for Ricoeur a form of ordering the world by the imagination. In narrative, he says, it is *plot* which serves the same function of productive invention, or of ordering the world in this way: plot '"grasps together" and integrates into one whole and complete story multiple and scattered events, thereby schematising the intelligible signification attached to the narrative as a whole' (Ricoeur 1984: x).

NARRATIVE AND HERMENEUTICS

Thus the aim in Ricoeur's work on narrative – consisting mainly of the three-volume *Time and Narrative* (*Temps et récit*, 1983, 1984 and 1985), and various of the studies in *Oneself as Another* (*Soi-même comme un autre*, 1990) – is again a *hermeneutic* one: 'whether it be a question of metaphor or of plot', he writes, 'to explain more is to understand better' (Ricoeur

1984: x). In the case of plot, understanding 'is grasping the operation that unifies into one whole and complete action the miscellany constituted by the circumstances, ends and means, initiatives and interactions, the reversals of fortune, and all the unintended consequences issuing from human action' (Ricoeur 1984: x). From this description it may be seen that two further aspects of narrative are important to Ricoeur: first, that like metaphor it involves *mimesis* in the sense of its representing human reality in some way; and second, the kind of reality that narrative is mimetic of is human *action*. Understanding human action through understanding mimesis is the aim of Ricoeur's work on narrative. Again, as with his work on metaphor, the ultimate goal is to discover the kind of human truth that scientific propositions cannot reach. This is a question of how we organise our own lives: the end-point of Ricoeur's lengthy analyses is to demonstrate that 'time becomes human time to the extent that it is organised after the manner of a narrative' (Ricoeur 1984: 3). In other words, we understand our own lives – our own selves and our own places in the world – by interpreting our lives as if they were narratives, or, more precisely, through the work of interpreting our lives we turn them into narratives, and life understood as narrative constitutes self-understanding. In his book *Oneself as Another*, Ricoeur goes on to develop the theory of narrative begun in *Time and Narrative* into a full-blown ethics, as we shall see in Chapter 6.

THE HEALTHY CIRCLE

Narrative is dependent on *time*: in order for there to be narrative, there must not only be events, but events following one after the other (*plot* is the ordering of those events, and the establishment of causal relationships between them). Just as in other areas of hermeneutic activity, or even just as in hermeneutics itself, Ricoeur discovers a 'healthy circle' – this time, between time and narrative: 'the world unfolded by every narrative work is always a temporal world . . .; narrative, in turn, is meaningful to the extent that it portrays the features of temporal experience' (Ricoeur 1984: 3). But Ricoeur invites us to see this circle rather as a spiral: each time the circle is turned, the same point is passed *at a higher level*, and so the grand hermeneutical project of reaching human understanding through self-understanding attains ever greater heights.

TIME

What then is time? That is the question posed in Book XI of St Augustine's *Confessions* (*c.* 397). Leaving aside the *scientific* theories of time initiated by Einstein's theory of relativity, there are essentially two *philosophical* theories of time. The first is the 'rationalist' theory, first advanced by Aristotle in his *Physics*, and developed by the German philosopher Immanuel Kant in the late eighteenth century. This sees time as a series of 'nows', a series of points each of which passes away to give rise to a new point in a succession. For Kant, time, like space, is an *intuitive a priori*: '*a priori*' meaning that the fact that time exists must be accepted *before* we can go on to make deductions about anything else whatever, and 'intuitive' meaning that we just *know*, as part of the human condition, that time exists – it is not something that can be *proved*.

The alternative theory of time is first advanced in the late fourth century by St Augustine. Although modern phenomenology was unknown to Augustine, this might be called the 'phenomenological' theory of time, since it is the theory accepted and developed by Husserl and Heidegger in the twentieth century. This theory starts by pointing out the *aporias* (gaps) in the understanding of time resulting from the Aristotelian theory: if time is a series of 'nows', then whenever I say *now*, the time of that now has already gone: whenever I try to isolate the present, it is already in the past. The perception of time – or, more particularly, of the *present* time – always lags behind the present time, the 'now'. The paradox is that the word 'now', which refers to the present, can never actually refer to the present, since as soon as the word is uttered, it is in the past. This is not just a problem with the

ST AUGUSTINE OF HIPPO (354–430)

St Augustine was, through such works as *De Doctrina Christiana* and *City of God*, one of the principal contributors of doctrine to the late ancient Church, but he is best known for his *Confessions* (*c.* 397), an autobiography of his first forty-one years, telling of his conversion to Christianity, and being addressed directly to God as the putative reader. The *Confessions* are wide-ranging, addressing such issues as the constitution of nature, the nature of mind, and the relation of religious belief to reason. His meditation on the nature of time in Book XI is often taken to be a model of philosophising.

word 'now', but is a problem about how the 'present' is perceived: on the one hand, we want to say that the present is always present, but on the other hand, as soon as we try to isolate it as present, it's gone – it's in the past. In mathematical terminology, the now-point of the present 'lacks extension'; it is an infinitely small point.

The result is a paradox whereby the present does not exist, if by 'exist' we mean that we can say of it, it *is*. We cannot point to the present and say '*this* point in time *is*, it *exists*', in the same way that we can say 'this table exists'. In fact, the same is true of the past and of the future: the future does not exist, because it has not happened yet; the past does not exist because it is not happening *now*; and *now* does not exist because it is never *now*. Although this sounds paradoxical, it does accord, for example, with our common-sense view of history: Alexander the Great, although he was a real person, does not exist in the same way that I exist, and this is not just because he is dead, but because he is a historical character; likewise, if you are reading this book 100 years from now (*my* 'now'), you do not exist in the same sense that I do. And this is why the problem of time is important for Ricoeur: there is still such a thing as *historical truth*, even though the past does not *exist* in the sense of 'having being'. And the truths of history are important truths, as the debate over those who wish to deny the Holocaust testifies.

The solution – if it may be so called – to this paradox for Augustine is a notion of the 'threefold present'. The past and the future exist in the mind, through memory on the one hand and expectation on the other. To conceive of the past and of the future, the mind must be stretched – *distended* – and Augustine's neat formula is that the lack of *extension* of the present is overcome by the *distension* of the mind. In fact, that is what thinking consists of: so long as the mind is thinking, it is thinking as what Heidegger called a 'presencing', a continuous stretching of the present mediated by memory of the past and expectation of the future. The continuous present contains the past and the future within it, so long as the mind is distended in this way, and a thinking mind is always distended in this way, since this is what thinking consists of.

This in turn allows a contrast between time and eternity. Eternity is not 'a very long time'; on the contrary, it is *outside* of time, it is not-time. It is part of the human condition to be trapped within time; when God created the world, He created time, and time will come to an end when the world does. God Himself is not bound by time; unlike man, He is time-less. The ancients recognised that time was intimately connected with the movement of objects: without time, there would be no movement. Augustine's stroke of genius is to declare that time is produced by the movement of the mind. We have been speaking of the 'mind', but for Augustine there was no distinction between the 'mind' and the 'soul'. The Latin word *anima* covers both modern meanings – and if a thing or person is *animated*, then of course it moves. The mind of God does not move – it is eternal. If a person's mind could be 'seized and held still', then that person would see what eternity looks like, but unfortunately for us, we are (unlike God) *created* beings, and so we cannot hold the mind still in this way other than by dying. But we can strive to imagine what eternity looks like – we can have that *inentio* (intention). The paradox (another paradox!) is that the mind strives harder and harder – moves faster and faster – in an effort to attain the peace that is eternal stillness. But that is the mental agony consequent upon being a fallen creature.

From this description of Ricoeur's description of Augustine, we can see why Augustine's theory of time is attractive to Ricoeur, and is the model he adopts in describing the time on which narrative depends. Ricoeur's formula is *intentio in distentio*, the dialectic between the intention of the mind towards stillness and the distension of the mind that constitutes its movement in time and thus constitutes the perception of time itself. The 'intention' of *intentio* is, for Ricoeur, phenomenological intention, or intentionality – it is the motivating force of the mind that *animates* meaning. If meaning comes from movement (the unfolding of words in sentences and sentences in discourse – no word has meaning in isolation), then meaning is produced and understood within time. Moreover, this is *human* time, understood as Augustine's 'threefold present', and it is *human* meaning, *animated*, having a soul. Narrative is the form of discourse which, through its dependence on plot, is richest in human meaning. Discover the meaning of narrative, and you discover the eternal truth of the human soul.

MIMESIS₁, MIMESIS₂ AND MIMESIS₃

As in his analysis of metaphor, Ricoeur adopts Aristotle's definition of mimesis: it is not (as it is in Plato) an imitation of nature, but an imitation of an action. This is why mimesis is intimately connected with *muthos* (emplotment), since emplotment orders not events, but actions, and conversely characters within narratives would have no motive to act were it not for the causal connections that emplotment provides. Plato's model of mimesis may be appropriate to painting or sculpture, but poets and authors open up the world of 'as if', and it is Aristotle's definition of mimesis, as involving *muthos*, which allows this: it 'produces the "literariness" of the work of literature', and 'opens the space for fiction'. Ricoeur goes further than Aristotle, however, and sees mimesis as a threefold process. He calls the three components of mimesis 'Mimesis₁', 'Mimesis₂' and 'Mimesis₃' respectively. Each of these three aspects of mimesis corresponds to each of the aspects of the 'threefold present' that constitutes time in Augustine's theory.

Mimesis₁ is *prefiguration*. By this, Ricoeur (1984: 54) means that 'some preliminary competence' of what human action consists of 'is required' in order to comprehend a plot. For example, we need to be able to identify who the *agent* (the person performing the action) is, and we need to be able to guess what this person is capable of doing; in fact, in approaching a plot we are already asking such questions as 'what', 'why', 'who', 'how', 'with whom' and 'against whom'. We ask these questions because we have what Ricoeur (1984: 55) calls 'practical understanding', that is, we know how people behave in the real world based upon our day-to-day experience within it. Narrative composition is anchored in our practical understanding, says Ricoeur, which is why someone without much experience of the world is likely to make a bad novelist, and why we are always dissatisfied if, in a film say, a twist in the plot is resolved through a character acting implausibly or inconsistently. We expect characters who act to have *motives* for their actions. In fact, Ricoeur identifies three ways in which we have a *preunderstanding* that we bring to narrative in interpreting it, or that a writer must have in order to compose it: they are *semantic* understanding (how one understands, for example, that 'X did A to B because of Y'), *symbolic* understanding (how one understands, for example, that the hero should be interpreted as a *good* character – 'good' is the symbolic value of 'hero'), and *temporal* understanding (how one understands, for example, that a character *is expected* to do something as a result of such-and-such an event having occurred to her). Mimesis₁, then, is the preunderstanding of narrative.

Mimesis₂, meanwhile, 'opens the kingdom of the *as if*' (Ricoeur 1984: 64), or the kingdom of fiction. It is a work of *configuration*, or of *muthos*, emplotment. Emplotment organises the various elements of a narrative into 'an intelligible whole' (Ricoeur 1984: 65). This is not merely the same as organising events into a series; rather, it is the 'thought' of the story, that which stops us asking 'But so what?' The incidents cannot merely be stuck together; they must be *related* in some way. That is not to say that incidents cannot be widely divergent in their nature, but nevertheless there must be some reason or purpose behind their occurring one after the other. Moreover, 'agents, goals, means, interactions, circumstances, unexpected results' (Ricoeur 1984: 65) are all brought together by emplotment.

As with Mimesis$_1$, there is also a *temporal* dimension to emplotment, concerned with what the literary critic Frank Kermode called (in his 1966 book of the same title) the *Sense of an Ending* – meaning attaches to a story because it is going somewhere, and it is from the end-point of a story that the story and its meaning can be seen as a whole. For Ricoeur, this temporal dimension to Mimesis$_2$ is what links it to Mimesis$_1$, which also has a temporal dimension. In Mimesis$_1$, we have a preunderstanding that a character might be expected to act in a certain way in a certain situation; in Mimesis$_2$ we can see whether or not the character did act in that way, and the reasons for their choice in terms of their contribution to the whole story. But we as readers can only do this by looking back over the story from the end-point. Narrative as a whole has an advantage over the characters within it, and over real-life people such as ourselves, precisely in that it can be re-read in this way. If Mimesis$_2$ grasps together the elements of the plot, then the reader is implicated in this grasping-together; the reader must also perform a work of reading in order to make this happen. (In a disjointed work such as James Joyce's *Ulysses*, which self-consciously plays with the sequencing of the events it describes, the reader has to do *most* of the work in this respect.)

This brings us to Mimesis$_3$, *refiguration*, which is 'the intersection of the world of the text and the world of the hearer or reader' (Ricoeur 1984: 71). It is the *application* of the world of the text to the real world. Aristotle would have said that poetic composition *teaches* us something, and something analogous could be said of works of narrative in general. There is a *point* to reading or hearing a narrative that reaches out beyond the narrative itself. In this dimension, Ricoeur's expansion of Aristotle's mimesis is closest to Plato's concept of mimesis as representation, except that it is not nature that is represented, but human

life. If narrative did not have this *referential* function, its purpose would
be lost, and we would not 'understand' it in any deep sense.

EMPLOTMENT

Of the three components of mimesis – Mimesis$_1$ (prefiguration),
Mimesis$_2$ (configuration) and Mimesis$_3$ (refiguration), Mimesis$_2$, or configuration, is the most important, because it is the dimension of mimesis that comprises *muthos*, or emplotment. Emplotment, says Ricoeur
(1984: 45), 'opens the space for fiction', and 'produces the "literariness"
of the work of literature'.

Emplotment *mediates* between Mimesis$_1$ and Mimesis$_3$. But *how* does
it do this? Let us call Mimesis$_1$ our understanding of the world that we
have already, and that we bring to the narrative in order to understand
it. And let us call Mimesis$_3$ the understanding we have of the world after
we have read the narrative (it is still mimesis, because our understanding
of the world now encompasses the narrative within it). We have turned
full circle: we have brought understanding of our world to the narrative, in order to understand the world. But this is a 'healthy' circle (it's
the hermeneutic circle once again), since our understanding is now
increased, taking in as it does the world of the text as well as our world,
the world of the reader.

This increased understanding is dependent on time. Ricoeur's (1984:
54) formula is that the understanding of narrative follows 'the destiny
of a prefigured time that becomes a refigured time through the
mediation of a configured time'. This dense formula needs unpacking.
Prefigured time is the time of our prior understanding – our understanding prior to engaging with the narrative. Refigured time is our
subsequent understanding – the new understanding of the real world
we have as a result of having read the narrative and understood it (the
real world, of course, encompassing the narrative within it). The configured time is the emplotment, the time of the narrative that orders its
events and incidents into a plot. Hence plot is what enables us to understand narrative as narrative, and as mimetic of the real world; it enables
us to see the actions depicted in a narrative as *human* actions.

Moreover, narrative time has the same threefold composition as time
experienced by humans, phenomenological time, except that it is its
mirror image. In narrative, prefiguring is configured into refiguring,
while in real life the present is an anticipation of the future mediated by

the memory of the past. It is because narrative time and real time mirror one another that the 'healthy circle' between narrative and real life exists: we can understand narrative because we understand life, and our understanding of life is increased by our understanding of narrative. Ricoeur's further turn of the circle – the hermeneutic circle, or circle of understanding – is constituted by the explanation of time within life and within mimesis, thus explaining *why* it is the case that mimesis + time = narrative, and *why* it is the case that narrative as such, and not Aristotle's divisions of poetic composition into tragedy, comedy and epic, is important to human life and its understanding.

HISTORY

It is Ricoeur's thesis that history is to be understood as a form of narrative. Both historical and fictional narrative have something in common, and that is that they are not *simply* lists of events. In fiction, 'The man drank hemlock. The man died' is not a narrative, but 'The man drank hemlock and then he died' is, since it is implicit that the man's dying is consequent on his drinking hemlock. Analogously, in history a list of events would be a mere chronology. History draws causal connections between events, it explains them: 'To explain why something happened and to explain what happened coincide. A narrative that fails to explain is less than a narrative. A narrative that does explain is a pure, plain narrative' (Ricoeur 1984: 148).

This said, there is nevertheless a fundamental difference between history writing and fiction (aside from the fact that in history, the events which comprise it are not invented). This difference lies at the level of emplotment: the ordering of events in history is imposed, whereas the fiction writer can manipulate them as she wishes. For Ricoeur (1984: 175), what history and fiction have in common is that they both require narrative competence – 'our ability to follow a story'. However, for the historian, writing history is a form of inquiry: the causal relations between events are explained explicitly, rather than being implicit in the form of the narrative itself: 'for historians, the explanatory form is made autonomous'; 'historians are in the situation of a judge: . . . they attempt to prove that one explanation is better than another' (Ricoeur 1984: 175). Unlike the fiction writer, who explains *by* recounting, the historian 'set[s] up the explanation itself as a problem in order to submit it to discussion and to the judgement of an audience' (Ricoeur 1984:

175). Unlike narrators of fiction, the historian has to contend with the problems of objectivity and truth. History is a 'scientific' discipline insofar as it aims at the truth and deals with historical facts, but the very act of interpreting those facts in the name of truth leaves open the way for alternative explanations, and thus destroys objectivity.

There is, then, what Ricoeur (1984: 179) calls 'a gap . . . between narrative explanation and historical explanation': narrative explanation is implicit to the narrative itself, whereas historical explanation, while forming an integral part of our understanding of history, is made autonomous by the historian. But does this not jeopardise the entire project of calling history a 'narrative'? After all, Ricoeur has already characterised narrative as a threefold mimesis, with Mimesis$_2$, emplotment, being the mediator between our prefigured understanding of how narratives work through how life works, and our reconfigured understanding of how life works through our understanding of the particular narrative in question. For history to be a narrative, emplotment must have an equally important place within it, and yet, because history writing separates out the explanation of the events of history from their sequential ordering, it looks as if emplotment, if it still may be called such, looks very different in history writing than it does in other kinds of narrative. After all, the events of the historian's 'plot' are selected from a pre-existing stock of facts, whereas the events of fictional narrative are invented by the author.

Ricoeur's solution to this problem is to call the elements of emplotment in history writing *quasi*-characters, *quasi*-plots and *quasi*-events. The quasi-characters of history are peoples, nations and civilisations, which 'serve as the traditional object between all the artefacts produced by history and the characters of a possible narrative' (Ricoeur 1984: 181). So, if history *were* a narrative, it would have characters in it, but instead we find peoples, nations and civilisations, which behave in history writing *as if* they were characters, and it is this *as if* behaviour of peoples, nations and civilisations in history writing that leads history back from being a science to being a narrative. Individual people have a 'participatory belonging' to these groupings of peoples, nations and civilisations, and it is through the presentation by history of the collective behaviour of these groupings that the agency (the ability to *bring things about*) of the individuals within them is expressed. Thus, historians attach 'singular causal imputations' to these quasi-characters; in other words, they provide causal explanations for their behaviour *as if* they were explaining the behaviour of single individuals. It is these causal explanations that give history the appearance of having plot; they are quasi-plots. Moreover, the events that happen in history are not sudden or brief, as everyday events are. They unfold over time, being brought about by the collective will, or agency, of the quasi-characters, and they have duration (since it lasted six years, the Second World War was not an 'event' in the same sense that Brutus stabbing Caesar was an event). Thus, the events of history are quasi-events. Between them, quasi-plot, quasi-character and quasi-event constitute what Ricoeur calls 'historical intentionality', the meaning-intention behind history to *be* history, as opposed to any other form of discourse.

Peoples, nations and civilisations have a historical permanence about them, unlike the particular individuals that may comprise those entities. History writing is at its most authentic when it explains what constitutes the 'existential continuity', or *tradition*, of these entities. Peoples, nations and civilisations are *first-order entities* within history writing, that is, they are the stuff that history writing is directly about. On the other hand, because their stories can be told tragically, in a manner employing the direct strategies of emplotment found in fiction writing, writing about the 'heroes' of history – people like Alexander the Great, Napoleon, or Bismarck – is the kind of history writing furthest from the project of authentic history, since it is the furthest from the 'quasi' of 'quasi-plot', 'quasi-character' and 'quasi-event'.

It is thus on this term 'quasi' that Ricoeur's theory of history rests. As he puts it:

> The term 'quasi' in the expressions 'quasi-plot', 'quasi-character', and 'quasi-event' bears witness to the highly analogical nature of the use of the narrative categories in scholarly history. In any event, this analogy expresses the tenuous and deeply hidden tie that holds history within the sphere of narrative and thereby preserves the historical dimension itself.
>
> (Ricoeur 1984: 230)

FICTION

Ricoeur calls fictional narrative any narrative that is not history: it 'includes everything the theory of literary genres puts under the rubrics of folktale, epic, tragedy, comedy and the novel'. Fictional narrative differs from historical narrative in the truth claim it makes under

Mimesis₃: in history, we reconfigure a world that we know to be 'true' in the sense that the actions explained really did happen and the explanations for them are plausible, whereas in fiction we take the narrative to be 'true' insofar as the working-through of the explanation that we as readers must perform in some sense deepens our understanding of our own lives.

Ricoeur's study of fictional narrative is deliberately confined to the study of Mimesis₂, or emplotment. Fictional narrative 'enriches' the concept of emplotment in a way historical narrative does not. Ricoeur recalls his original definition of 'emplotment' as a 'grasping together' or 'configuration'; more particularly, it is a configuring *act*. This act is, says Ricoeur (1985: 61), a kind of 'reflective judgement': 'to narrate a story is to "reflect upon" the event narrated'. If this is so, then 'narrative "grasping together" carries with it the capacity for distancing itself from its own production and in this way dividing itself in two' (Ricoeur 1985: 61).

There are three interdependent ways in which narrative fiction performs this work of dividing itself from itself in order for it to be self-reflexive. The first is at the linguistic level: narrative fiction forces a distinction between *statement* (what is being said) and *utterance* (the way in which it is being said), and this it does through its employment of verb tenses. *Discourse* typically employs variations on the present tense (e.g. with continuous aspect), or (for those languages that have a future tense) the future: 'I'm just going to the shops'. *Narrative*, by contrast, typically employs past tenses, and especially the 'aorist' or 'preterite' tense (in modern Anglo-American parlance, the simple past): 'The man drank the hemlock and then he died.' Now, verb tenses do not necessarily coincide with the division of time into the past, present and future: there is often a mismatch between statement and utterance when it comes to verbs. For example, English (unlike French) has no future tense, and typically constructs future statements from utterances involving a modal plus an infinitive ('I will go . . .'). Ricoeur wants to claim that in narrative fiction, there is *always* a mismatch between the verbal utterance and the statement made thereby, or at least, the verb tenses always mean two things at once: they simultaneously mean that the narrative is taking place in the past of the narrator, and that the narrative is taking place in some sense in the real past of the reader. Although the work is fiction, it is still significant that in real time as well as in narrative time the events *have happened* rather than *are happening* or *will happen*, otherwise it would not be typical to use the past tenses for narratives. And the significance lies in the link forged between the fictive world of the narrative and the real world: again, it is *as if* the events of the narrative have happened in the past. Thus the employment of past tenses in fiction is one of the ways in which the transition from Mimesis$_1$ to Mimesis$_2$ is achieved.

The second way in which narrative fiction divides itself from itself is in its manipulation of time (a process which, of course, is achieved through the use of verbs, among other parts of speech). An example of the manipulation of time in fiction is to be found in Henry Fielding's novel of 1749, *The History of Tom Jones, A Foundling*. As Ricoeur (1985: 78) puts it, 'As a master, conscious of playing with time, [Fielding] devotes each of his eighteen books [of *Tom Jones*] to temporal segments of varying lengths – from several years to several hours – slowing down or speeding up, as the case may be, omitting one thing or emphasising another.' There is, then, a distinction here between *narrating* time and *narrated* time. Narrating time moves at a steady pace, as is witnessed by the fact that the reader reads at the same steady pace – three pages of Book II, for example, will take the same amount of time to read as three pages of Book XVII. Narrated time, meanwhile, alters its pace depending on what the narration imposes upon it, so that three pages of one part of the novel might cover a few minutes of the time of the story, whereas three pages of another part of the novel might cover several years. Thus, within the time of narrating, narrated time is unequally distributed.

What makes this division possible is the ability to measure the work of fiction, and it is significant that Fielding was the first novelist to divide his works into books and chapters as understood in the modern sense. But Ricoeur's (1985: 78) next question is 'if we measure something, just what are we measuring?' He admits that narrating time is conventionalised – it is merely an assumption that it takes the same amount of time to read one page as it does another. But admitting this convention, we can still nevertheless 'say that narrating requires "a fixed lapse of physical time" that the clock measures' (Ricoeur 1985: 79). When comparing narrating time with narrated time, then, what is being compared are 'lengths' of time, which are measured in hours and minutes in the first case, and years, days, hours and minutes in the second. But merely comparing chronologies in this way would not be very interesting if all it revealed was that narrated time is just a compressed version of narrating time. What is interesting about narrated time is the other things the narration does with time: it skips over dead time, for example, or condenses duration into a single speech event ('every day', 'unceasingly', 'for weeks', 'in the autumn', etc.). In other words, a *tempo* or *rhythm* is established in fictional narrative, and this allows the reader to see the work as a whole, as a *Gestalt*. So, although the comparative measurements of narrating time and narrated time form the basis of understanding time in fictional narrative, they provide the opening into other features, and it is these other features which allow the reader to grasp together the time of the narrative as a whole.

The third and final way in which fictional narrative divides itself from itself in order to become self-reflexive is through point of view and narrative voice, which create a distinction between narrator and character. Ricoeur has already defined mimesis as mimesis *of action*. But you cannot have action without acting beings, or *agents*. Ricoeur (1985: 88) says that 'acting beings are . . . beings who think or feel – better, beings capable of talking about their thoughts, their feelings, and their actions'. This being so, it is 'possible to shift the notion of mimesis from the action toward the character, and from the character toward the character's discourse'. This brings us back to the earlier distinction between utterance and statement: 'the utterance becomes the discourse of the narrator, while the statement becomes the discourse of a character' (Ricoeur 1985: 88). Point of view and narrative voice are the means by which this is brought about.

Point of view is the means by which consciousness is presented in fiction; it is a mimesis of consciousness. This is because fiction allows the narrator to enter the minds of the characters; the characters have an 'inner transparency' to the omniscient narrator. Of course, this is a matter of choice of style: the author might choose to allow his narrator to see into the mind of only one of the characters, or of none at all. But omniscience of the narrator is a possibility in principle inherent to fictional narrative, and this regardless of whether the narrative is third-person or first-person: in this latter case, the narrator speaks 'as if' they were someone else in describing their past speech and feelings. Linguistically, point of view may be conveyed through various means: direct speech, indirect speech and 'free indirect speech', whereby it is apparent that the words are to be taken as a character's thoughts, although this is not explicitly announced by the narrator. Whatever, it is 'the major property of narrative fiction . . . that it produces the discourse of a narrator recounting the discourse of fictional characters' (Ricoeur 1985: 93). It is this property which allows at once distance between the *author's* point of view and that of his narrator and the characters, and facilitates the promulgation of the author's point of view in the ordinary sense of his opinion, or his ideology. This the author can do either by expressing positive evaluations of the characters through the mouth of the narrator, or the reverse – or even by having an unsympathetic narrator pass negative judgements on characters of which the reader would approve. But why is all of this called 'point of view' in the technical sense of the perspective from which the characters and events of a story are presented to the reader? The answer, for Ricoeur, is first that the characters and events are literally *seen* by the narrator; it is this which orientates the reader in space, the space or world of the novel. Second, the narrator has *temporal* perspective: just as he can move about in space, so too can he shift in time:

> The narrator may walk in step with his characters, making the present of narration coincide with his or her own present, and thereby accepting the limits and lack of knowledge imposed by this perspective. Or, on the contrary, the narrator may move forward or backward, considering the present from the point of view of the anticipation of a remembered past or as the past memory of an anticipated future, etc.
>
> (Ricoeur 1985: 94)

Narrative voice is similar to, but not the same as, point of view. 'The narrator is', says Ricoeur (1985: 96), 'the fictive author of the discourse'; he is the means by which the real author projects himself into the text. According to Ricoeur it is theoretically possible to have a story with no point of view at all – presumably this would involve a narrator who had no powers of omniscience, and who merely recorded events without evaluating them, or describing the psychologies of the characters involved. But it is impossible to have a story without a *narrator* at all, and therefore it is impossible to have a story without narrative voice. On the other hand, it *is* possible to have a story with more than one narrative voice, or with the narrative voice being distributed among various characters – this is the case, for example, with Wilkie Collins' *The Woman in White* (1860). The various narrative voices may actually engage in dialogue with each other, or, as is the case with Fyodor Dostoevsky's fictional diarist in *Notes from the Underground*

(1864), with the reader: 'Now, are not you fancying, gentlemen, that I am expressing remorse for something now, that I am asking your forgiveness for something? I am sure you are fancying that . . . However, I assure you I do not care if you are' (Dostoevsky 1972: 15). The more narrators there are, the more the concept of 'mimesis of action' gets stretched, so that a completely 'polyphonic' (many-voiced) novel such as Virginia Woolf's *The Waves* (1931) 'is no longer a novel at all but a sort of oratorio offered for reading' (Ricoeur 1985: 97). Although *The Waves* is a very effective mimesis of consciousness, it is no longer narrative fiction, and is therefore not mimetic of consciousness *of time*, which is where Ricoeur's concern lies.

How are these three ways in which narrative is divided from itself connected to one another? The answer, for Ricoeur, lies in the privilege attaching to the preterite – the simple past: it is 'the privileged signal of the entry into narrative' (Ricoeur 1985: 98); it immediately tells the reader, 'you are about to read a story'. And it has this privilege because the reader understands that the story is in the past from the perspective of the voice telling it, which means that the reader also understands that the narrator is *posterior* to, comes after, the story. Understanding the tense that the narrative is framed in is therefore a prerequisite to understanding the point of view and voice adopted by the narrator. Voice and point of view are, in turn, that part of the narrative that addresses itself to the reader: they are 'situated at the point of transition between configuration and refiguration, inasmuch as reading marks the point of intersection between the world of the text and the world of the reader' (Ricoeur 1985: 99). So, verbal tense marks the intersection between Mimesis$_1$ (prefiguration) and Mimesis$_2$ (configuration), and voice and point of view mark the intersection between Mimesis$_2$ (configuration) and Mimesis$_3$ (refiguration).

HISTORY AND FICTION TOGETHER

So far, Ricoeur has explained historical narrative and fictional narrative separately; his next step is to show how refiguration, or Mimesis$_3$, works. To do this he demonstrates how the 'referential intentions' – the ways in which these works are intended to represent the truth – of historical narrative and fictional narrative *interweave*. The purpose of this demonstration is to show how the 'world of the text' is made complete by the 'life-world of the reader'.

An initial problem, however, is in the distinction between historical time and fictional time – Ricoeur may have explored each individually, but he has not said how they differ from one another. The obvious difference lies in the reality of the historical past, as contrasted with the unreality of the fictional past. If the task is to describe how historical narrative and fictional narrative interweave or intersect, this difference must first be reconciled.

Ricoeur begins this task by arguing that the 'reality' of 'historical reality' should not be understood naïvely. What do we mean when we say that the historical past is *real*? There is a conundrum to understanding the historical past, insofar as it once was real in the same sense as the book you are now holding is real, but that reality has now disappeared. Yet we want to say that the historical past is real. According to Ricoeur, the reality of the historical past survives in what he calls 'traces', which consist of testimonies, documents, witness-accounts, etc., and in the memories of individuals. The trace is the persistence of the past through its vestiges in the present. But it is not just the persistence of the past as such, but of past people. Typically, traces of the past consist of the works of people. History is, precisely, the reworking of these traces into a re-presentation of the past in our present. We do this out of a sense of debt to the dead: without them, we would be creatures cast adrift from any sense of continuity – we owe our being as cultured humanity to those who have gone before. History is the payment of this debt. Many historians would see themselves as *constructing* history in their writings, but in this work of construction they are also *reconstructing* the reality of the past. The constructions of the historian have, says Ricoeur (1988: 100), a relationship of 'standing-for' or 'taking the place of' 'a past that is abolished yet preserved in its traces'. History cannot be understood other than as the persistence of the past in the present; history re-enacts the past by re-presenting its traces. It is in this way that history is to be understood, and not directly as having a *referential* function (i.e. its consisting of a series of statements of the truth).

Seen in this way, however, history would appear to be an 'abyss' away from fiction: we have no sense of debt towards the past characters of a fictive work and, moreover, fiction's ability to play games with time seems diametrically opposed to history's need to maintain faith with tradition and continuity. What bridges this abyss for Ricoeur is the act of reading, which reveals key similarities between history and fiction at strategic points. First, there is a link at the level of the author. The author of history is constrained by the facts he works with: he constructs only insofar as he arranges them plausibly; he does not invent them. The fiction author, meanwhile, has the freedom to invent. But Ricoeur points out that this is not merely a 'freedom from . . .', but also a 'freedom for'. The 'law of artistic creation' is, Ricoeur claims, as 'stringent' for the artist as is the rule of historical facts to the historian. The law of creation 'is to render as perfectly as possible the vision of the world that inspires the artist', and this 'corresponds feature by feature to the debt of the historian and of the reader of history with respect to the dead' (Ricoeur 1988: 177).

Second, the act of reading itself has features in reading fiction which are analogous to the process of reading history (*analogous*, but not the *same*). Fiction brings before the reader an implied author; the work of fiction is to lead the reader to believe that the implied author is identical with the reader himself – such is the 'expectation of the text'. But the reader resists this tendency, through bringing to the text their own cultural knowledge – such is the 'expectation of reading'. So, the text tries to 'suspend the reader's disbelief', as the Romantic poet Samuel Taylor Coleridge would have put it, while the reader simultaneously goes along with this, and *knows* she is being led in this direction. The structure of this negotiation between accepting the text and distancing oneself from it has, Ricoeur wants to claim, the same structure as the relation of 'standing for' between history and the reality of the past.

Third, we 'read in common'. Why do great works (of fiction) have canonical status? Because, despite differences between people over time, a large group of people continue to recognise the work's capacity to generate ever new meanings and new interpretations. Despite the differences individual readers have, they all recognise that great works have *something* that makes them great. This 'appeal structure' of great literature is, in its ability to be universal, analogous to the appeal of history to repay our debt to the dead.

Fourth, and finally, the reading of history and the reading of fiction both change social reality; put simply, in both cases readers are likely to go out and change the world as a result of what they have read. This, though, happens in quite a different way in the experience of reading fiction than it does in reading history. Fiction has the effect of making readers 'unreal' insofar as they enter into the world of the fiction; they 'emigrate' their minds to the world of the text, at least for a while. Paradoxically, it is those works that are the farthest removed from actual reality that are the most likely to change the world through affecting the reader – because they require the greatest leap of the imagination.

But Ricoeur does not want merely to argue that history and fiction have things in common – he claims they are *interweaved*: 'on the one hand, history in some way makes use of fiction to refigure time and, on the other hand, fiction makes use of history for the same ends' (Ricoeur 1988: 181). History borrows two things from fiction. First, it makes use of techniques of composition (operating at the level of configuration): 'history imitates in its own writing the types of emplotment handed down by our narrative tradition' (Ricoeur 1988: 185). But second, and more importantly, history also involves something at the level of refiguration, and that is what Ricoeur (1988: 185) calls 'the representative function of the historical imagination. We learn to see a given series of events *as* tragic, *as* comic, and so on.' It is this which makes great history books as perennial as great novels: 'a history book can be read as a novel' (Ricoeur 1988: 186). When this is the case, says Ricoeur, a complicity develops between the narrative voice and the implied reader; our guard is lowered, and we come to have trust in the work: as Ricoeur (1988: 186) puts it, we succumb 'to the hallucination of presence'. But there is another way in which history is fictionalised. That is when history tells of 'epoch-making' events, that is, events which a community holds to define their origin. Historians are supposed to set aside their own feelings, but when those events are close to us, history takes on a new ethical purpose. That purpose is to convey admiration or, more importantly, in the case of events that have victims, horror (Auschwitz being a case in point). It is the duty of history (to the victims) to convey the horror of epoch-making events, and yet horror is not itself a category of history, but of fiction: Ricoeur (1988: 188) says, 'fiction gives eyes to the horrified narrator'. It is in this final interweaving of fiction within history to form narrative that we see the importance of narrative as such: 'There are perhaps crimes that must not be forgotten, victims whose suffering cries less for vengeance than for narration. The will not to forget alone can prevent these crimes from ever occurring again' (Ricoeur 1988: 189).

If fiction is interweaved in history, then history is also interweaved in fiction. Fictional narrative imitates historical narrative insofar as it recounts events *as if* they were past: 'Fictional narrative is quasi-historical to the extent that the unreal events that it relates are past facts for the narrative voice that addresses itself to the reader. It is in this that they resemble past events and that fiction resembles history' (Ricoeur 1988: 190). The past that fiction describes is a probable past, a past that 'might have been'. There is what Ricoeur calls a 'deep affinity' here between the fictive past and the real past, in that the real past is full of unrealised possibilities. Fiction pursues an alternative time line to the one that reality has actually taken. Fiction may be free from the constraints of the 'traces' of history – documentary proof – but it still has an obligation to its 'quasi-past', and that is an obligation to the artist who suffered in creating it. Fiction pays the debt the reader owes to the artist's suffering, in the same way that history pays the debt the reader owes to the dead.

SUMMARY

For Ricoeur, narrative is mimetic of human action. There is a healthy hermeneutic circle between narrative and life – narrative imitates life and we can learn about life from narrative – and in turning this circle the under-standing of life is continuously elevated. Narratives are exemplary of a model of time, but this is human, or phenomenological, time, and not time conceived as a series of points. Just as human time is experienced as an anticipation of the future through the retention of the past in memory, so narrative consists of a three-stage mimesis, no one stage of which makes sense without the operation of the other two. Mimesis$_1$ is *prefiguration*, the pre-understanding we have of what narratives consist of that we bring to a text in reading it. Mimesis$_2$ is *configuration* or *emplotment*, the ordering of events and the establishing of causal and other relations between them. Mimesis$_3$ is *refiguration*, the act of reading whereby our understanding of the world is increased by the new slant on it that the narrative has provided. Narratives require readers to complete them; the reader provides Mimesis$_3$, without which Mimesis$_1$ and Mimesis$_2$ would be without purpose.

There are two types of narrative: history and fiction. Despite their differ-ences, they have things in common: they each show a human truth rather than a referential truth, and they both require the same sort of 'narrative competence' in order to be understood. Peoples and nations in history writing behave *as if* they were characters in a fiction, just as characters in fiction behave *as if* they were real people, and the past of fiction is depicted *as if* it were the real past that history depicts. Ricoeur seeks to demonstrate, however, that history and fiction not only have things in common, but are *interweaved* in the narrative experience of life. We understand history as events that are tragic, and historical characters as heroic, for example, and it is in this way that history repays our debt to the dead. Conversely, it is because fictional accounts are related *as if* they were historical that we can learn moral lessons from them.

6

ETHICS

Ricoeur (1992: 172) defines the ethical intention as 'aiming at the "good life" with and for others, in just institutions'. This definition distinguishes ethics from morals, morals being the adherence to laws or rules of behaviour. Ricoeur's enquiry, rather, is into *virtue ethics*; it is an enquiry into what it means in general to *be* a good person – what virtues one must possess – rather than an enquiry into 'applied ethics' or 'moral philosophy', which attempt to decide whether certain actions (abortion, euthanasia, waging war, etc.) are 'good' or 'bad', either in absolute terms or in certain situations. The 'aiming at' part of the formula 'aiming at the "good life"' is also, we should remember, a narrative journey: the good life is a life worthy of being recounted. This is the ethical aim of Ricoeur's own work on narrative, or indeed of his whole life's work. The analysis of the mimetic structures of narrative, of time in narrative, and of the relationship between fiction and history, are all of value in and of themselves, and each casts new light on the discipline of which the analysis forms a part – literary criticism, historiography, etc. But the real purpose of these analyses is to demonstrate the narrative dimension of human life itself, which justifies hermeneutics not only as a process of reading texts, but of reading lives. If hermeneutics is the route to understanding, then reading oneself is the key to self-understanding. If literary judgement is an ethical judgement (books are not only good or bad aesthetically, but also morally), then the same may be said of the judgements made of a life recounted.

NARRATIVE IDENTITY: *IDEM* AND *IPSE*

If in living my life I *configure* it as a narrative, I understand my life by *refiguring* it: 'the fragile offshoot issuing from the union of history and fiction is the assignment to an individual or a community of a specific identity that we can call their narrative identity . . . To state the identity of an individual or a community is to answer the question, "Who did this?", "Who is the agent, the author?"' (Ricoeur 1988: 246). And the answer to this question of 'Who?', if it is to be more than merely a proper name, 'has to be narrative':

> To answer the question 'Who?' . . . is to tell the story of a life. The story told tells about the action of the 'who'. And the identity of this 'who' therefore itself must be narrative identity.
>
> (Ricoeur 1988: 246)

What, then, does 'identity' mean in this context? Latin has one word for 'identity' understood as 'being the same' (*idem*), and another word for 'identity' understood as 'oneself as self-same' (*ipse*), and for Ricoeur it is this latter, *ipse* meaning of 'identity' which constitutes narrative identity, and the identity of a person. *Ipse* means 'self-constancy'; unlike the 'sameness' of *idem* it can include change 'within the cohesion of one lifetime' (Ricoeur 1988: 246). I am the 'same' person I was twenty years ago, even though I am so much different, and it is this sameness-in-difference that is my *ipse*, my narrative identity: 'As the literary analysis of autobiography confirms, the story of a life continues to be refigured by all the truthful or fictive stories a subject tells about himself or herself. This refiguration makes this life a cloth woven of stories told' (Ricoeur 1988: 246).

Ricoeur's argument regarding narrative is here brought full circle. Initially, he claimed that we have a *pre-understanding* of narrative, and it was this pre-understanding that we bring to narratives when we interpret them. Now, Ricoeur is asking what it is that makes us have a pre-understanding of narrative. The answer to this question is a 'chain of assertions' which together encapsulate more or less the entirety of Ricoeur's philosophy of life: 'self-understanding is an interpretation;

interpretation of the self, in turn, finds in the narrative . . . a privileged form of mediation; the latter borrows from history as well as from fiction, making a life story a fictional history or, if one prefers, a historical fiction, interweaving the historiographic style of biographies with the novelistic style of imaginary autobiographies' (Ricoeur 1992: 114). And what it is that narrative mediates between is *description* and *prescription*. In order to act, I must first describe the given situation in the world, then I must decide what I should do. 'Describe, narrate, prescribe' is Ricoeur's (1992: 114) formula for human action.

It follows from this that there is 'no ethically neutral narrative' (Ricoeur 1992: 115). Narrative *evaluates* situations and tells us what we *should* do, in a moral sense. Seeing our own lives as narrative, meanwhile, is what gives us a sense of '*connectedness of life*' (Ricoeur 1992: 117). But this concept depends on allowing some *idem* – sameness into the *ipse* – sameness of narrative identity. What is crucial about the 'sameness' of my life in terms of *idem* is the sense of permanence in time. 'This is how we see photos of ourselves at successive stages of our life', says Ricoeur (1992: 117): there is 'an ordered series of small changes' which 'threaten resemblance without destroying it'. The meaning of the word *same* in the sense of *idem* answers the question 'What am I?', and the meaning of the word *same* in the sense of *ipse* answers the question 'Who am I?'

CHARACTER AND KEEPING ONE'S WORD

As my life progresses, I change – not only physically but morally – but despite these changes, I am still the same person: I have (an) identity. The manner in which I change is my sameness (identity) understood as *ipse*; my constant sameness of bearing the same proper name to describe the same object that I am at any particular point in my life is my sameness (identity) understood as *idem*. In order to be a person, I must have both of these attributes – *idem* and *ipse*. According to Ricoeur, the place where these two attributes of identity come together is in *character*. Character, according to Ricoeur, is comprised of two *dispositions* (the way in which I am *disposed* to act in a certain manner). The first is *habit*, which 'gives a history to character' (Ricoeur 1992: 121). Each habit, once acquired, becomes a character trait, 'a distinctive sign by which a person is recognised, reidentified as the same' (Ricoeur 1992: 121). The second disposition which a character has is 'the set of *acquired identifications* by which the other enters into the composition of the same' (Ricoeur 1992: 121). By 'the other' here Ricoeur means other people – we recognise ourselves by identifying ourselves with other people, that is, by identifying with the 'values, norms, ideals, models and heroes' of communities of which we feel ourselves to be a part. We especially like to identify with heroic figures, because we share their values (or the other way round: it is because they share our values to an elevated degree that we consider someone 'heroic'), and this sense of identifying *with* someone inculcates a sense of loyalty and fidelity into our character, which again is a form of 'maintaining the self' (Ricoeur 1992: 121). This leads Ricoeur to emphasise the importance of *keeping one's word* as a way of demonstrating self-constancy. Although the self-constancy of keeping one's word is not the same thing as having character ('the continuity of character is one thing, the perseverance of faithfulness to a word that has been given is something else again' (Ricoeur 1992: 123), it is still a marker of the self's permanency in time. In fact, in some ways it is more important than character – 'continuity of character is one thing', says Ricoeur (1992: 123), 'the constancy of friendship is quite another'. Continuity of character is a prerequisite for a moral being, but if one keeps one's word, then one is *already* acting in a moral manner. A character having continuity may still lack friends, but keeping one's word creates friendship. (As we shall see in the next chapter, Ricoeur prefers friendship to erotic love.)

Ricoeur's (1992: 171) aim is to 'establish the primacy of ethics over morality'. By 'morality' he means the *norm*, or set of rules, that are established for us to be able to live our lives in a moral way. By *ethics* he means the *aim* of living a life that might be described as *good*. So, in privileging ethics over morality, Ricoeur wants to say that he is privileging the aim towards living a good life over an examination of *rules* which might be followed in order to 'be good'. If we want to live a 'good life', we have an 'ethical intention', and as we have seen this is defined by Ricoeur (1992: 172) as 'aiming at the good life with and for others, in just institutions'. But how will we know if a life has been 'good'? The answer is, by examining it, which really means, by reading it as if it were a story. Ricoeur is much impressed by Socrates' dictum that a life worth living is a life worth recounting. So, once again, there is a direct parallel between narrative and life. Life *is* a narrative: in living, we create the story of our lives.

So far Ricoeur's ethics has been highly dependent on narrative, and more particularly on narrative that is seen as an intermingling of the fictive and the historical. Within the fictive side of the equation, great privilege has been accorded *literary* fictions, as is demonstrated by Ricoeur's choice of various early twentieth-century novels to demonstrate the working of time in fiction. Indeed, Ricoeur often talks as if all fiction were literary fiction; at least, he sees literature as the highest form of the fictional. In this way, literature – especially the great novel – becomes an example, or a model, of how we might understand our own lives. Furthermore, when Ricoeur moves his analysis into questions of continuity of character and keeping one's word, literature becomes a model of how we might live a *good* life.

STORIES VERSUS LIFE

But here an objection is raised. It is the one stated by the narrative theorist Louis O. Mink (1970: 557–8), and repeated by Ricoeur on several occasions: 'Stories are not lived but told'. The counterpart to this is that 'Lives are not told, but lived'. The difference is again one concerning time, particularly the privileged temporal knowledge that the author of a story (or in Ricoeur's terms, the implied author as expressed through the narrator) has over people living their lives. The narrator of a story *knows* what is going to happen next, precisely because, as Ricoeur's analysis of narrative voice has pointed out, the time of a narrative is in the narrator's past – which is why the typical tense in which narratives are told is the simple past. People living their lives, on the other hand, do not know what is going to happen next. Therefore, it looks like quite a strong claim to say that we are authoring our own lives. We *can* do, if we write an autobiography at the end of our life. But that is not the same as claiming that we are actively authoring our lives as we live them. Apart from anything else, a real author of a fiction has control over all of the characters within the fiction and, indeed, of the whole world of the fiction. Individual people, on the other hand, have only limited control over the real world: they can control (but not absolutely) their own actions, but can at best influence the actions of others, and have no control at all over the contingencies of the world, such as so-called 'acts of God'. And yet another objection to seeing life as a narrative is that authored stories have *closure* – the entirety of a fictional character's life may be told by the narrator. Real people, on the other hand, cannot experience such closure, because they cannot look back on their own lives from a point after the moment of death. The understanding of my own life in completeness can only by undertaken by others.

THE STORY OF LIFE

For his theory that life itself is a narrative to work, then, Ricoeur has to overcome these essential differences between stories and lives. His first move is to point out that these objections do not rule out the *applicability* of narrative to life. For example, 'the narratives provided by literature serve to soften the sting of anguish in the face of the unknown, of nothingness, by giving it in imagination the shape of this or that death, exemplary in one way or another' (Ricoeur 1992: 162). So, although we cannot experience our own death in the full sense of seeing it retrospectively, and it may be this unknown aspect of death that is frightening, the examples of death in literature can console us to some extent.

But this still does not answer the objections that oppose life to narrative. Ricoeur's response is to acknowledge the objections to some extent, and turn them into beneficial modifications of the model of life as narrative. In terms of narrative's being a recounting of the past, Ricoeur reminds us that the past recounted in narrative is only the *quasi*-past of the narrator, and thus 'among the facts recounted in the past tense we find projects, expectations, and anticipations by means of which the protagonists in the narrative are orientated toward their mortal future' (Ricoeur 1992: 163). Thus narratives 'teach us how to articulate . . . retrospection and prospection'; we look to the past and anticipate the future – look to the past *in* anticipating the future – in the same way as is accomplished by narratives.

On the question of closure, narratives themselves, says Ricoeur, are not as closed as we might think, even if the death of the hero might be depicted in them. Not all narratives are written with the quasi-know-ledge of a character's death, or include that death, and in any case the narrative itself, whether it includes a death or not, is never in and of itself *closed* – as Ricoeur's analysis of narrative in terms of Mimesis$_1$, Mimesis$_2$ and Mimesis$_3$ has revealed, narratives require readers in order to arrive at closure. In the same way, the narrative of a life needs to be examined in order for it to be understood; it is the performing of the act of scrutinising the life that gives it closure, not death. And if the closure of a life is not *completed* by these means, well, then, neither is narrative closure completed by the act of reading, since new readings which lend new meanings to narrative are always possible.

Finally, life is like narrative in its *entanglements*. Of course it is true that in life, we are not entirely the authors of our own destiny in the same way that a fictive author has complete control over all of the characters and events in his book. But even though stories are narrated from the point of view of a single character, they are never solely *about* a single character. Even a monologue such as those devised by the modernist playwright Samuel Beckett (1906–89) recounts other characters along the way. Within a story, there are strands of narrative, and these all intersect with each other – telling the story from one character's point of view means telling the story from the point at which the various strands of narrative have intersected with that character. Life can be seen in the same way. I am telling a story from my point of view. But that does not mean that other characters are not involved. On the contrary, without other characters, I would have no life story to tell. My life is a narrative thread, which interweaves with the narrative threads that are the lives of others. Sometimes there will be a dense interweaving, as with other people I come to know well; at other times there will be the simplest crossing of threads, as in a chance encounter.

'HERE I AM!'

This brings us to what is for Ricoeur the main ethical point of seeing life as a narrative, and that is that it does not allow people to be seen in isolation. Establishing personal identity as narrative identity is a way of locating self-constancy in life, but self-constancy conceived in this way cannot help but involve other people. I demonstrate my self-constancy by being constant to my word – my promise – to *others*. It is in this way that the interweaving of the narrative strands of the lives of others with the narrative strand of my own life comes to have ethical pertinence:

> Self-constancy is for each person that manner of conducting himself or herself so that others can *count on* that person. Because someone is counting on me, I am *accountable for* my actions before another. The term 'responsibility' unites both meanings: 'counting on' and 'being accountable for'. It unites them, adding to them an idea of a *response* to the question 'Where are you?' asked by

another who needs me. This response is the following: 'Here I am!', a response that is a statement of self-constancy.

(Ricoeur 1992: 165)

Now, we remember that the passage from *idem* to *ipse* was the passage from 'What am I?' to 'Who am I?', and that this passage was achieved, according to Ricoeur, through the mediation of narrative. Once we reach, through our responsibility to others, the stage of saying 'Here I am!', the distinction between 'What am I?' and 'Who am I?' becomes irrelevant. The gap between 'What am I?' and 'Who am I?' constitutes narrative identity; the constancy involved in declaring 'Here I am!' constitutes moral identity. There is what Ricoeur calls a 'fruitful tension' between narrative identity and moral identity: narrative identity gives rise to moral identity, *despite* its constituting a questioning of the self, whereas moral identity looks like a confident assertion. The questioning of narrative identity keeps the assertion of moral identity in check: 'Here I am!' is not the boast of a braggart, but an expression of humility by an individual who has made himself at the disposal of another. 'Here I am!' is an expression of care.

SUMMARY

Ricoeur's ethics is a version of virtue ethics. It seeks not to scrutinise which particular deeds are good or bad, but rather to consider what constitutes a 'good life'. Ricoeur follows Socrates' dictum that a good life is a life worth recounting. This draws a direct parallel between life and narrative: for Ricoeur, life *is* a narrative. In life, I have what Ricoeur calls a 'narrative identity'. 'Identity' here is identity in the sense of *ipse* rather than of *idem*. In other words, despite my being a different person in terms of both physical and moral attributes at different times of my life, I am still the 'same' person. I maintain this sameness of my personhood by having self-constancy; it is this that constitutes my 'character'. Self-constancy is expressed through keeping one's word. Despite the changes that may happen in my life, if I keep my word to others, I show myself still to be the same person, and I am of 'good character'.

But there is an objection to the theory that life is a narrative, and that is that 'lives are lived; stories are told'. The fact that morally good stories may serve as a model for real lives is a hint that this objection may be overcome.

The objection is overcome by understanding 'narrative' not in a naïve way, but in the way analysed earlier by Ricoeur in terms of Mimesis$_1$, Mimesis$_2$ and Mimesis$_3$. Just as literary narratives require the work of readers (Mimesis$_3$) to complete them, so real lives require others to interpret them. It is the interpretations of others, and not death, that brings closure to the narrative of life. Moreover, my life is entangled with others' lives. Each of these individual lives can be seen as narrative threads within the great plot of life: sometimes the threads are knotted together, sometimes they merely cross. In order to have narrative identity, I must interact with others: with no other people in my life, I would have no life story to tell. The ethical way of interacting with others is also the way that preserves my own constancy of character, and hence my own narrative identity – it is in keeping my word. In making a promise, I am saying that the other can count on me, and it is this which makes me accountable. Thus in my proceeding to moral responsibility, the philosophical questions that children are likely to ask, 'Who am I?' or 'What am I?', become replaced by the assertion 'Here I am!', which is an expression of care for the other, of putting oneself at another's disposal.

7

POLITICS AND JUSTICE

Thus far we have examined Ricoeur's ethics in terms of the self and of others. But we recall that his definition of 'the ethical aim' was 'aiming at the good life with and for others, in just institutions' (Ricoeur 1992: 172). We must now look at what constitutes 'justice', and hence 'just institutions', for Ricoeur. The phrase 'just institutions' should serve as a clue that for Ricoeur, justice and politics are inextricably intertwined.

'THE POLITICAL PARADOX'

Ricoeur's arguably most celebrated political essay, 'The Political Paradox', dates from 1957. The 'paradox' of the title refers to the fact that power is a necessary means of furthering the aims of politics, which is the same as the aim of philosophy, to expand the sum of happiness and the good. On the other hand, power inherently lends itself to perversion and abuse, and hence to the opposite of good, evil. More specifically, Ricoeur's central question is, how could the phenomenon of Stalin be possible under a socialist regime? If socialism stands for the treatment of all equally, how could socialism be maintained by a tyrant, or, conversely, how could a tyrant exercise the perversion and abuse of power under the name of socialism?

The answer, according to Ricoeur, stems from a fundamental error in the philosophy of Marxism. That error lies in treating all alienation

MARXIST POLITICAL ECONOMY

According to Karl Marx (1818–83), capitalism 'alienates' the worker from the means of production. In a pre-capitalist society, the worker works essentially for himself, and is directly motivated in his labours by the quality of the goods he produces, which can be exchanged for other goods of similar quality. Under capitalism, the worker falls victim to machine technology: he is no longer held responsible for the production of a 'good', but merely contributes to the *process* of its manufacture. Moreover, his motivation is no longer the direct exchange value of the finished product of his labours, but the value of his labour itself, as sold to the capitalist at an unfair rate. The direct link between the worker and the absolute value of the goods he produces is broken, and it is this that constitutes his alienation. The solution to this problem, according to Marx, is the overthrow of the capitalist class by the working class, who themselves take over the means of production and thus enjoy directly the exchange value it affords, which is distributed equally between the members of that class.

to be economic alienation. Ricoeur points out that Marx's solution to the problem of economic alienation, a solution which was attempted by the Soviet Union, conflates economics (the alienation of the workers from the means of production) with politics (the seizure of control of the state by the workers). But it does not follow that if a worker, or any member of society, is economically alienated they must be politically alienated, or vice versa. Thus in the Soviet Union, under the dictator Joseph Stalin, the political *end* of abolishing economic alienation was achieved, and wealth was distributed equably among the working class, but political alienation was not abolished as a consequence. On the contrary, ordinary people were so far alienated from the political process that they faced the Gulag, or disappearance, if they dared voice an opinion. This is not, says Ricoeur, true merely of socialist states, but of any state whatever: 'no state exists without a government, an administration, a police force; consequently, the phenomenon of political alienation traverses all regimes and is found within all constitutional forms' (Ricoeur 1965b: 259). There is a contradiction at the heart of the political state as such, however it is constituted. On the one hand, it pretends to universality, in other words, that it represents all of its citizens equally, and it claims to treat them all equally, in a *rational* manner. On the other hand, all states in practice act with 'particularity and caprice' (Ricoeur 1965b: 259), owing to the power they have, as states, over their citizens – in practice, they behave *irrationally*. It is this kind of irrational action which defines 'political evil' for Ricoeur: 'political "evil" is, in the literal sense, the madness of grandeur, that is to say, the madness of what is great – grandeur and culpability of power!' (Ricoeur 1965b: 261).

If state power is a necessary evil, the evil must be curbed:

> The problem of the control of the state consists in this: to devise institutional techniques especially designed to render possible the exercise of power and render its abuse impossible. The notion of 'control' derives directly from the central paradox of man's political existence; it is the *practical* resolution to this paradox. To be sure, it is, of course, necessary that the state should *be* but that it not be too much. It must direct, organise, and make decisions so that the political animal himself might be; but it must not lead to the tyrant.
>
> (Ricoeur 1965b: 262)

For Ricoeur, the notion of the 'withering away of the state', as promulgated by the leader of the Russian Revolution, Vladimir Lenin (1870–1924), is a 'myth'. This is not to say that Lenin was not sincere. He saw the state under capitalism as an organ of repression; therefore, it followed, if the workers are to take the means of production into their own hands, this cannot be accomplished without the working class also taking over the functions of the state – this is what Lenin means by 'the dictatorship of the proletariat'. As Ricoeur (1965b: 263) summarises,

> if the armed populace is substituted for the permanent army, if the police force is subject to dismissal at any moment, if bureaucracy is dismantled as an organised body and reduced to the lowest paid condition, then the general force of the majority of the people replaces the special force of repression found in the bourgeois state, and the beginning of the withering away of the state coincides with the dictatorship of the proletariat.

But the state did not wither away under Communism – it got stronger than ever! Ricoeur posits various reasons for this. First, the socialist state confuses 'the administration of things' with 'the governing of persons', as was shown in their 'five-year plans', which not only determined what should be produced and how it should be distributed, but also who should do the producing and in what way. Second, the socialist state continued to be like capitalism insofar as, contrary to the promise of Marx's collaborator Friedrich Engels (1820–95), work did not become a joy, but continued to be a burden, and the state became obliged to 'motivate' the workers not by the distribution of the wealth gained from their production, but by such means as intimidation, the threat of violence, deportation, etc. Third, the socialist state saw the future in terms of generations – what was being done to society was for the benefit of that society's grandchildren. This allows the state to discontinue treating the present generation with respect, and moreover reintroduces 'alienation' into people's lives, albeit in a different form. And finally, 'the socialist state is more ideological than the "liberal" state' (Ricoeur 1965b: 266). This means that it controls not only the means of production, but also propaganda, etc. – in other words, it seeks to control the inner world of people's minds as well as their external circumstances.

SOCIALISM WITHOUT A SOCIALIST STATE

Ricoeur's conclusion from this critique of the socialist state is that the state cannot wither away as Lenin claimed it would. The alternative to its withering away, then, must be to control it. It is Ricoeur's contention that the state can only be controlled within a 'liberal' state, not within the state of 'actually existing socialism' that was to be seen during the Soviet era. Since he sees himself as a socialist, this is quite a bold intellectual move on Ricoeur's part. But it is Ricoeur's contention that it is possible to attain a socialist economics within a liberal politics. His socialism is, then, a non-Marxist socialism; in fact, one could go so far as to describe Ricoeur as anti-Marxist. For him, the fault – the evil – of the Marxist socialist state (i.e. the Communist state) is that there is no room in it for public opinion (he points out that it was the Soviet state, not the people, who denounced Stalin). Public opinion is expressed through multiple political parties, and this is what Ricoeur means by 'liberal' when he declares his support for the liberal state. The liberal state is a *pluralist* state, and socialism should be argued for within a political framework that allows for other, opposing views.

The other advantage of the liberal state – another curb on the necessary evil of its power – is its lawfulness. In a socialist state, the law is merely the instrument of the state. It is this which allows the socialist state to exact 'a violence without appeal' (Ricoeur 1965b: 255). But in a liberal state, the law is seen as in some sense above the state – the citizen can appeal to the law in the face of the state's attempt to exercise power unreasonably. This is what is meant by the term 'a state *founded on* law': law, the rule of justice, is seen as prior to the state, and the state as such is as answerable to it as is any of its citizens. Ricoeur sees this as being the 'admirable idea' behind the eighteenth-century French philosopher Jean-Jacques Rousseau's *Social Contract*: the state provides 'not the exchange of savage liberty for security, but the passage to civil existence through law which is given the consent of all' (Ricoeur 1965b: 252).

JUSTICE VERSUS VENGEANCE

Ricoeur takes up the theme of the political again at the end of the 1980s, over thirty years after the publication of 'The Political Paradox', and throughout the 1990s publishes a series of lectures and articles on the relationship between politics and justice. His return to the theme of the political is motivated by an interest in justice, which in turn is born out of his work on ethics. Moreover, in the 1950s the prominent question was of how socialist states could behave in a totalitarian manner, when socialism professes to be democratic in its ideology. But with the fall of Communism in the late 1980s, a new philosophical problem appeared on Ricoeur's intellectual horizon: if liberal democracy has been adopted as the global model for the conduct of society, what are the responsibilities of the citizen within that society, both to other citizens and to the state? Ricoeur sees this as no longer being a problem of the relationship of economics to politics, but a problem of the relationship of *justice* to politics.

Why do we feel that it is *unjust* for the weakest members of society to be sacrificed for the greater good? Ricoeur (2000: x) says that 'indignation in the face of injustice' comes in advance of what we consider to be justice. Every child feels keenly a sense of injustice done to them, as is manifested in the cry 'That's not fair!', and this sense is felt before any positive feeling of justice. Ricoeur (2000: xi) summarises the motives behind such childhood indignation: they are 'disproportionate retributions, betrayed promises, [and] unequal shares'. This feeling of indignation marks, says Ricoeur, our first entry into the rule of law, which has as its counterparts to these three childhood motivations 'penal law, the law of contracts and exchanges, [and] distributive justice' respectively.

But in adult life we are not content with mere indignation at injustice; we seek positive justice. To attain justice, though, we must overcome the desire for vengeance. Vengeance is not justice. There are two features that justice must have in contrast to vengeance. First, the retribution must be less severe than the crime. 'An eye for an eye' is not justice, it is vengeance. This is what many victims of crime find difficult to accept – they are still at the level of indignation at the injustice suffered by themselves as victims, rather than having reached a stage of accepting justice. This leads to the second quality of justice, that it requires the intervention of a third party – most simply, a judge, and then, by extension, a whole judicial system of courts, juries, etc. This apparatus of the third party is necessary to justice, because if we were to allow punishment to be decided by the victim, we would be back with the vengeance of 'an eye for an eye'. The third party acts as a mediator between the criminal and the victim, setting a *just distance* between one and the other, being as they are (or should be) impartial. To summarise, then, justice for Ricoeur is not the simple inverse of injustice, although it might find in injustice its initial motivation: 'just distance, the mediation of a third party, and impartiality present themselves as the great synonyms of a sense of justice along the path down which indignation has led us from our earliest youth' (Ricoeur 2000: xi).

AGAINST UTILITARIANISM

Ricoeur's theory of justice is anti-utilitarian. Utilitarianism as a philosophy can be summarised in a single slogan: the greatest good for the greatest number. The consequence of a society adhering to this utilitarian principle is that every individual must make a personal sacrifice in order to maximise the good of the whole. This means that the extent of the sacrifice is proportional to the distance from the median point; more simply, the further you are from the average, the more you have to sacrifice. Hence those at the extreme edges of society have to sacrifice the most: this is fine for the very wealthy ('wealthy' means wealthy in 'social goods', which are not solely economic, but extend to rights, freedoms, and similar intangibles) who can afford to sacrifice much, but not so for those at the other extreme, who find themselves divested of their goods altogether. Ricoeur's objection to utilitarianism is that it relies on a 'sacrificial principle', and in so doing, the weakest members of society are sacrificed to the greater good. The weakest members of society are victimised, are turned into scapegoats. This is clearly an injustice, but Ricoeur's task is not merely to feel indignation at this injustice, but to develop a positive theory of justice in the place of utilitarian theory.

THE GOLDEN RULE AND THE NEW COMMANDMENT

As a starting point in developing his theory of positive justice, Ricoeur contrasts the 'golden rule' with the 'new commandment'. The 'golden rule' is to be found in the Gospel according to Luke (6:31): 'Treat others as you would like them to treat you.' The 'new commandment' originally appears in Leviticus, and is repeated in Matthew 22:39: 'Love your neighbour as yourself.' In *Oneself as Another* Ricoeur (1992: 219) had already pointed out that the 'golden rule' establishes a 'norm of reciprocity' between the agent and the patient (the person acting and the person acted upon). But in his work subsequent to *Oneself as Another* Ricoeur wants to point out not only the similarities, but also the differences, between the 'golden rule' and the 'new commandment'. According to Ricoeur (in the essays 'The Golden Rule: Exegetical and Theological Perplexities' (1989), and 'Love and Justice' (1991)), the 'golden rule' is a commandment to justice, whereas the 'new commandment' is a commandment to love. The difference lies in the fact that the reciprocity of the golden rule implies an equality between the parties concerned: if I treat others as I would wish them to treat me, then that presupposes that they will treat me as I would treat them, creating a social contract between equal parties. The formalisation of this in law as a rule of justice would be 'treat similar cases in similar ways'. But the 'new commandment' has a *logic of superabundance* rather than a *logic of equivalence*: it is a logic of generosity whereby I give more than the other deserves in relation to me, and not merely an amount equivalent to that which I will receive in return. If the 'golden rule' is ethical, then the 'new commandment' is hyperethical – more ethical than the ethical – and that, after all, is what love is. It is 'an extreme form of commitment' (Ricoeur 1996a: 35).

The problem with the 'golden rule' is that it is open to a perverse interpretation, and that is that 'I will only do this for you if you do something for me'. The 'new commandment' acts as a 'corrective' to this

JOHN RAWLS (b. 1921)

In his highly influential *A Theory of Justice* (1971), Rawls adopts a 'game theory' of social organisation. According to this theory, each player seeks to maximise the minimal share (this is called the 'maximin' principle for short). This theory opposes both Marxism and utilitarianism. It is anti-Marxist, because it does not presuppose that all shares be equal, either as a starting point or as an outcome. And it is anti-utilitarian, in that the *minimum* share, rather than the maximum ('the greatest good of the greatest number') is the starting point. Rawls' theory is often called a *distributive* theory of justice, because it advocates distributing shares of 'goods' to the members of a society (remembering that 'goods' are intangibles such as freedoms and rights as well as material goods). It is also a *contractual* theory of justice, because it imagines for the sake of argument that there is a *social contract*, or agreement between members of a society to behave towards one another in a reasonable way according to the rule of law. Rawls distils his theory into two principles:

First: each person is to have an equal right to the most extensive basic liberty compatible with a similar liberty for others.

Second: social and economic inequalities are to be arranged so that they are both (a) reasonably expected to be to everyone's advantage, and (b) attached to positions and offices open to all (Rawls 1972: 60).

(Incidentally, Rawls' biggest influence in the political sphere is on British Prime Minister Tony Blair. The New Labour policy of 'social inclusion' is an attempt to put Rawls' second principle into practice.)

possible interpretation. Ricoeur's purpose in drawing this distinction between the rule of justice and the rule of love is to posit a theory of justice that avoids utilitarianism. This theory is essentially borrowed from the work of the philosopher of law John Rawls. Ricoeur is drawn to Rawls because the latter, too, is more interested in *virtue ethics* than in 'morality': 'Justice is the first virtue of social institutions' (Rawls 1972: 3). Ricoeur's analysis of the distinction between the 'golden rule' and the 'new commandment' is also an analysis of Rawls' principles of justice, and an attempt to show *why* Rawls' theory avoids utilitarianism:

What saves Rawls' second principle of justice from falling into . . . utilitarianism is finally its secret kinship with the commandment to love, inasmuch as the latter is directed against the process of victimisation that utilitarianism sanctions when it proposes as its ideal the maximisation of the average advantage of the greatest number at the price of the sacrifice of a small number, a sinister implication that utilitarianism tries to conceal.

(Ricoeur 1996a: 36)

Love, then, and justice are mutually dependent on one another. A justice without love is not true justice, but one which accepts the sacrifice of the weakest. Conversely, justice is the medium through which love is expressed. It is through just social institutions that I can love my neighbour as myself; love in the sense of *agape* (brotherly love), as opposed to *eros* (erotic love). Ricoeur prefers brotherly love to erotic love because the former is based on an ethics of superabundance – giving to the other person while expecting nothing in return. Erotic love, on the other hand, is based on desire, and as the French psychoanalyst Jacques Lacan (1901–81) often said, 'desire is the desire to be desired'. Desire demands a reciprocal relation between two equals, whereas in friendship the agent makes no such demand of the patient.

In day-to-day life, the 'new' commandment to love is a commandment to let go of the principle behind the cry 'It's not fair!'. We could say that the commandment to love aims towards an *adult* sense of justice. Ricoeur sees the path towards true justice as traversing three concentric circles. The first circle is that of vengeance – 'an eye for an eye'. The second circle is that of the 'golden rule', whereby vengeance is replaced by justice: 'Justice encounters its contrary first in the thirst for vengeance, which is a powerful passion: justice consists in *not* seeking vengeance' (Ricoeur 1998: 117). The third circle is that of the 'new commandment', whereby love replaces justice. Or rather, it *dis*places it: just as I surrender vengeance if I agree to be bound by justice, so also I surrender justice (for myself) if I agree to be bound by love. More particularly, justice in the sense of claiming one's share of the 'arithmetic equality' is surrendered in favour of allowing a share to the other person. I allow justice to the other person by surrendering my own desire for it.

THE GIFT AND PARDON

Justice obeys what Ricoeur calls the 'economy of the gift'. The economy of the gift differs from the economy of exchange insofar as nothing is expected in return on the part of the person giving. In terms of justice, says Ricoeur (1996a: 33), 'justification . . . is . . . a gift inasmuch as it is a free pardon'. Without the acceptance on the part of the wronged party that they will not receive an eye for their eye, that the punishment will not quite measure up to the crime, justice would not be justice, but vengeance. There is thus a paradox at the heart of the concept of justice, insofar as it does not entirely negate an injustice. This is particularly so in the treatment of murder in those countries which have abolished the death penalty. Life imprisonment is not death; the difference between the two constitutes a remainder which the wronged party (or her friends and relatives) must accept as members of a civil society based on the rule of law. In this way, law comes to be the formalisation of the commandment to love my neighbour or enemy; it is the formal mechanism whereby both this positive commandment is enforced just as much as the negative commandments of the 'thou shalt not' type. All justice, then, requires at least a degree of pardon on the part of a victim of a crime. Pardon is thus like love, or even is an aspect or expression of love itself, since 'it stems from an economy of the gift, in virtue of the logic of superabundance that articulates it and that has to be opposed to the logic of equivalence presiding over justice' (Ricoeur 2000: 144).

AMNESTY

But Ricoeur is careful to draw a distinction between pardon and amnesty. Pardon can never be *expected* of the victim, and is often, rightly, refused – some wrongs are simply 'irreparable' (Ricoeur 2000: 144). Pardon is, rather, an overlooking of the debt, a healing of memory, rather like the end of mourning. If pardon is a healing of memory, then memory is necessary to pardon, whereas amnesty is a kind of forgetting, and thus a 'heavy price to pay' (Ricoeur 2000: 143). Amnesty is a 'caricature' of pardon,

> since it purports to erase the debt *and* the fact. Amnesty . . . is an institution-alised form of amnesia. Today, for example, you do not have the right to say that a particular general stationed in Algeria was a criminal: you can be sued for defamation because amnesty was declared. It is true that . . . amnesty contributes to the public tranquillity that forms one of the responsibilities of the state. In this way, in certain cases, public tranquillity can imply amnesty; the slate is wiped clean. But with all the dangers that forgetting presents:

permanent forgetting, amnesia. Amnesty is a constitutional power which
should be used as infrequently as possible.

(Ricoeur 1998: 126)

'It is a question of a veritable institutional amnesia that invites us to act
as though something never happened' (Ricoeur 2000: 143). Ricoeur,
on the contrary, believes in the duty to remember. Collective remembrance constitutes history. If pardon is a gift, then it is tied to memory
in that when something is given, there is a debt on the part of the recip-
ient. Unlike in exchange economy, in the economy of the gift nothing
is given in return. Pardon remembers this fact that nothing is given in
return; it remembers that through the magnanimity of those granting
pardon (the victims of a crime), the crime has been forgiven. 'Forgiven'
is not the same as 'forgotten': amnesty erases this distinction between
forgiving and forgetting in a way that pardon does not.

In discussing narrative, Ricoeur said that history should be recounted
out of duty to the dead. In the political sphere, Ricoeur claims that
history – as collective memory – should be recounted out of duty to its
victims (who may still be alive). The forgetting entailed by amnesty is an
attempt to erase history, and is therefore unethical because it abnegates
the duty to remember. But why is there a duty to remember? The
Marxist would say that 'whoever does not learn from history is condemned to repeat it', but this is not, or is not primarily, Ricoeur's
response. Rather, he is more concerned with the concept of *responsibility*. An amnesty for criminals removes the sense of responsibility for their
crimes that attaches to them. But this dehumanises the criminal as much
as the criminal may have dehumanised his victims, since it is the definition of a free human being that he has responsibility for his actions as an
agent. Moreover, the judge, as third party that establishes a judicial distance between the criminal and the victim, also has a responsibility to the
victim. If through accepting justice the victim must give up vengeance,
then the least that can be done is that the victim does indeed get justice.
If the crime is forgotten through amnesty, then the victim gets nothing,
and that is not only not vengeance, but it is not justice, either.

OVERCOMING THE 'POLITICAL PARADOX'

All of Ricoeur's remarks about justice apply not only to the justice
gained or meted out by individuals living within the law. They are, more

importantly, applicable to how society as a whole is governed. When Ricoeur speaks of 'history' and 'responsibility', he does not mean merely the history of an individual and of some one person who may have wronged that individual. He is also speaking of 'the level of peoples and nations' (Ricoeur 1996b: 10). For example, the Holocaust is an example of the duty never to forget on the part of the collective memory that is history. Although the victims of the Holocaust perhaps cannot forgive the crimes perpetrated against them, the German author- ities were right to seek forgiveness during the post-war period. It is precisely by *not* forgetting that forgiveness can be asked, and sometimes granted, and this on a world historical level as well as on the level of the judicial system of a particular country affecting its citizens. At the level of the individual, forgiveness by, say, royal pardon is an act of charity, as a result of the pardoner being 'moved to pity' (Ricoeur 1996b: 12) the criminal being punished. At the level of states and peoples, 'forgiveness is the best way of shattering the debt, and thus of lifting impediments to the practice of justice and recognition' (Ricoeur 1996b: 12).

This connection between justice and society is to be found even at the level of the act of judging itself. We might think that the act of judging is a private matter performed by a judge for the benefit of the victim and the accused. But for Ricoeur, it is important that the act of judging be seen to be part of the public sphere. Returning to Rawls' idea that society is 'a vast system for distributing shares', Ricoeur (2000: 129) says that 'the exercise of the act of judging easily finds a place in the general functioning of society':

Taken in a broad sense, the act of judging consists in separating spheres of activity, in delimiting the claims of the one from those of the other, and finally in correcting unjust distributions, when the activity of one party encroaches on the field of exercise of other parties.

(Ricoeur 2000: 129–30)

When it comes to the specific case of judging at the end of a trial, more- over, the judgement comes at the end of a process of 'conflict, differences of opinion, quarrels, litigation' (Ricoeur 2000: 130). In order to make a judgement, the judge must first deliberate, then make a decision, then pass judgement. In allowing this process, says Ricoeur (2000: 130), a society has chosen 'discourse over violence'. The act of judging at the end of a trial is a model for the governance of society insofar as the cry of vengeance – which is a cry for violence – of the aggrieved party has been replaced by the discourse that constitutes the act of judging: 'it turns out that the horizon of the act of judging is finally more than security – it is *social peace*' (Ricoeur 2000: 131). The act of judging, then, has two aspects: it is at once an act of separating two parties, of deciding between them, and it is also the means by which each of us shares in, or takes part in, society. It is because the act of judging places a 'just distance' between parties that 'the winner and loser of any trial can be said to have their fair share in that model of co-operation that is society' (Ricoeur 2000: 132).

A MODEL OF THE STATE

Having taken this lengthy detour through problems of justice, is Ricoeur any closer to formulating a political theory, in the broad sense of a theory of how society should be organised? Following the political philosopher Hannah Arendt (1906–75), Ricoeur draws a distinction between *power* and *authority*. In 'The Political Paradox' Ricoeur had analysed the fault of the socialist states of the Soviet era as lying in their confusion of economic organisation with political practice. Another way of stating the same fault is to say that the socialist states took power upon themselves. Power, says Ricoeur, should lie with the people. This power of the people is exercised in liberal democracies through the election of representatives, and through all of the paraphernalia of discussion, debate and opposition that this entails.

This power should not be confused with *authority*, which it is perfectly legitimate for the state to exercise. Authority consists, for example, in the juridical system – we can tell that authority is different from power, because the state itself is answerable to the law in democratic countries. The law has authority not because it has been *granted* it, but because it is *foundational*. In his lecture 'Power and Violence' (1989) Ricoeur reminds us that authority is handed down to us through tradition from the founding of the state as such. This is distinct from power, which 'in principle' lies with the people (Ricoeur forthcoming). (The Communist governments blurred the distinction between power and authority by claiming to *be* the people.) Ricoeur points out that after all political revolutions, there has been a *founding act* whereby the new political system has been invested with authority, and that that act is not only an action in the sense of a group of citizens doing something, but also an enactment in the legal sense.

Ricoeur's political ideal is one of *civic virtue*, whereby groups of citizens decide to live together. In order to live together, they must co-operate. The constitution is the written formalisation of the authority that the original citizens who founded the state invested in that state; the 'social contract' is the mutual recognition that citizens have for one another, mediated through this constitution. In recognising the constitution, citizens recognise one another – despite their differences, all groups agree to recognise the constitution.

The constitution, then, fulfils the same role in the state as does the process of judgement within the legal system. It is a replacement of violence by discourse. Despite the distinction Ricoeur makes between authority and power, they both have something in common, and that is that they have the potential of violence attaching to them. In the case of authority, as Ricoeur (1965b: 237) pointed out as early as his 1957 essay 'State and Violence',

> authority is that of the 'magistrate', that of justice. The 'order' which it engenders and maintains could not therefore be separated from justice, even less opposed to justice. But it is precisely this established violence, this violence of justice which constitutes a problem.

As far as justice entails punishment, it is opposed to love: justice must be tempered by love in order to be ethical, and this is manifested in the judicial system by the exercise of pardon. Likewise, the potential for violence attaches to power. Power is political evil when it becomes power over other people. It too must be tempered by love when it is exercised. The safeguard against the abuse of power is a constant vigilance, which means a continual invocation of the constitution in the face of the state's arbitrary exercise of power over others.

The same principles of justice which guided founding fathers in founding states after revolutions must be constantly affirmed anew; it is the citizenry's responsibility to subject the state to a constant questioning as to the degree to which it exercises its power. This is what Ricoeur means by 'non-violence' and 'pacifism', principles in which he is a firm believer, despite his active service during the Second World War. 'Pacifism' does not mean a refusal to participate in the affairs of the state – a refusal to aid the process of war, for example. It means actively participating in opposition to the state's abuse of its own power, an abuse which comes from forgetting that it owes its power to the people as their representative. Hence Ricoeur is also in favour of *anti*-violence rather than non-violence, insofar as such an exercise of power by the state constitutes a return on its part to the violence of the seizure of power at its foundation, erasing the subsequent replacement of that violence by discourse in the form of a constitution. In short, non-violence means engaging the state in discourse – exercising freedom of speech. It is this that constantly re-creates us as citizens within democracies; under totalitarian regimes it requires a good conscience and self-sacrifice on the part of the individual citizen that is truly akin to the Christian *agape*, or brotherly love.

SUMMARY

Ricoeur identifies a 'political paradox': that the state is founded on rational principles, and yet in practice behaves arbitrarily and capriciously. The ability and tendency for states to act in this way is a result of the political power they have: political power is political evil. This is demonstrated by the example of the socialist states, which were supposed to wither away under Communism, but actually became more oppressive than ever. The answer to this conundrum is not a theoretical one, but a practical one. In practice, a liberal state that facilitates plurality of political parties is the best form of state, because it reduces political alienation through the expression of public opinion. Socialists should distinguish *political* alienation from *economic* alienation: a socialist economics should be argued for, and is achievable, within the framework of a liberal pluralist state.

Another reason for preferring the liberal state over the socialist state is that it is answerable to the rule of law. The rule of law is itself a template for the establishment of social justice. Justice replaces the violence of vengeance, in that it means that there is no longer equality of measure between the crime and the punishment. Moreover, acceptance of justice, as opposed to vengeance, by the victim is also an acceptance of the role of a third party (the judge) as mediator. And yet justice itself is still not enough for the Christian: justice must be tempered by love, which in practical terms means granting the gift of pardon. (Pardon is to be preferred to amnesty, since the latter entails a forgetting of the crime, which is unjust to the victim.)

Society, according to Ricoeur, is organised on a *civic* basis; it is a collection of social and other interest groups, with competing needs and aspirations. The aim of society should be to turn this competition into co-operation. Social groups behave in the same way as individuals behave before the law. Thus a state founded on law should act as the third party or judge, a mediator between the people and the goods (not only material goods, but also freedoms and responsibilities) that it has to distribute. It should distribute these fairly, which is to say justly, but this is not necessarily the same as *equally*. In distributing goods in this way a state exercises its authority, as distinct from power, which still lies with the people in a liberal state answerable to the rule of law. Just as individuals consent to submit to the law, so a state organised by rule of law governs by consent of the people. The constant vigilance of the people in asserting their constitutional rights is a guard against the state lapsing from exercising its authority to exercising power.

AFTER RICOEUR

Despite his contretemps with the French Government during the Algerian war of independence in the early 1960s, and again after the Nanterre affair, Ricoeur is the sort of academic who is likely to be made a Dean of Faculty, have prizes bestowed on him, be invited to dine with the Presidents of France and the US and spend his summer holidays with the Pope (all of which he has done) – in other words, he is something of an establishment figure, and so not a fashionable one. But there is a continuity between his biography and his intellectual work. Hermeneutics is a progressive discipline: each reading, whether it be of a text or of the texture of life, builds on previous readings rather than negating them. As a hermeneuticist, and as in life, Ricoeur is not an oppositional thinker: he would rather find the hidden 'secret communion' with apparently disparate beliefs (as he does with Freud in relation to phenomenology and religion) than set himself up as a destroyer of the arguments of others. Consequently, Ricoeur is happy to wear his own influences on his sleeve, and he is generous in acknowledging his sources: for example, to the historiographer Hayden White, the literary theorist Wayne Booth and the moral philosopher Alistair MacIntyre in his theory of narrative, or to the political philosopher John Rawls in his theory of political justice. This humility on Ricoeur's part tends to cast a shadow over his own influence, which is nevertheless significant in the fields of literary theory and theology, and particularly in the area where these two fields overlap, namely *biblical hermeneutics*, or Bible interpretation.

As a theory of interpretation, it might be expected that hermeneutics would have gained ready acceptance as a literary critical methodology. While this may have been true in France (as in the 'phenomenological criticism' of the critic George Poulet), for many years hermeneutic criticism did not really find favour in the English-speaking world. This is partly owing to an accident of history: Ricoeur's first collection of theoretical essays on hermeneutics, *The Conflict of Interpretations*, was published at the end of the 1960s, at about the same time that the work of Derrida was being popularised in the United States by the critic-philosopher Paul de Man, and others associated with Yale University. Deconstruction, transformed in the US from a philosophy into a literary critical methodology, became in retrospect the new orthodoxy in Anglo-American literary criticism (although at the time it looked like the radical challenger of the literary critical establishment). Ricoeur's hermeneutics was, during this period, condemned to live in decon-struction's shadow. Ricoeur's case was not helped by there being no examples of specific *literary* texts which had been subjected to Ricoeur's hermeneutics.

Interest in Ricoeur as a literary theorist began to take off in the 1970s on Ricoeur's decampment to Chicago and Toronto, and the publication of *Interpretation Theory* in 1976 and the English translation of *The Rule of Metaphor* in 1977. *The Rule of Metaphor* engaged with literary critics such as I. A. Richards, and privileged literature as the site not only of where metaphor was most likely to be located, but of where it was most likely to reveal truth. However, it was Derrida who was to have the last word in the debate on metaphor which Ricoeur's book generated.

DERRIDA, METAPHOR AND LANGUAGE

We recall from Chapter 4 that Ricoeur criticised Derrida's theory of metaphor, accusing Derrida of being a 'philosopher of suspicion'. According to Ricoeur's reading, for Derrida all metaphor is dead metaphor, and since all language is essentially metaphorical, all language is 'dead', in the sense that its users are led into a false belief that they are controlling it, while in reality the true meanings of words have been forgotten, and the *referential* function of language (its ability to refer to things in the real world) is always already, necessarily and irretrievably compromised. Consequently philosophy, as an activity expressed through the medium of language, deceives itself when it claims to arrive at incontrovertible truths.

In a lecture delivered some three years after the publication of *The Rule of Metaphor*, Derrida responds to the characterisation of his philosophy presented in Ricoeur's book. Derrida finds the notion of defending himself against Ricoeur's attack problematic, since he maintains that he is 'indebted' to Ricoeur, and that many of the claims he made in his original essay, 'White Mythology', were actually consistent with Ricoeur's positions: 'It is because I sometimes subscribe to some of Ricoeur's propositions', he says, 'that I am tempted to protest when I see him turn them back against me as if they were not already evident in what I have written'; and again: 'I am not in agreement with Ricoeur when he attributes statements to me in order to contest them with statements which I had begun by putting into question myself' (Derrida 1998: 107 and 109). But this does not mean that Derrida and Ricoeur are in *entire* agreement. If Derrida was already putting into question Nietzsche's concept of the dead metaphor and its catastrophic consequences for philosophical discourse in 'White Mythology', it does not follow that this putting into question leads to the opposite position, advocated by Ricoeur, that living metaphor is the lively expression that keeps philosophical discourse alive. Rather, Derrida wishes to question, or 'deconstruct', the received opposition between 'dead' and 'living', and not only between the *words* 'dead' and 'living', but also between the philosophical concepts that lie behind them. Instead of merely opposing to one another the concepts of dead and living metaphors, Derrida introduces the concept of a '*retrait* of metaphor'. The French word *retrait* means 'retreat', but is left untranslated to make visible its indebtedness to the word *trait*, which is lost in English. For Derrida, metaphor is constantly in retreat – each time a metaphor is coined, it begins to die. But this is a paradoxical process: it means that language becomes ever more metaphorical (in the Nietzschean sense that the words in any given language have lost their original meanings) and simultaneously ever less metaphorical (in the Ricoeurean sense that if a metaphor is dead, then it is no longer a metaphor – it is just language).

It is this self-contradictory double movement, or trait crossing its own path (re-trait), of language that fascinates Derrida, and precisely for a metaphysical reason. Heidegger pointed out that Being is a very peculiar 'thing', insofar as it is the only 'thing' of which we cannot say that it *has being*, which is why we must put 'thing' in inverted commas when we talk about Being – is Being a thing? We can say of beings that they have being, but we cannot say of Being as such that it has being. Derrida's inflexion on this problem is to point out that since Being 'itself' is nothing, is not a being, it cannot be expressed or named through the use of metaphor. 'And therefore', Derrida (1998: 116–17) goes on, Being 'does not have, in such a context of the dominant metaphysical usage of the word "metaphor", a proper or literal meaning which could be alluded to metaphorically by metaphysics. Consequently, if we cannot speak metaphorically on its subject, neither can we speak properly or literally.' This says something about both language and Being. Language cannot do without metaphor, since it is a condition of any piece of non-metaphorical language that there be a metaphorical usage to compare it to – this reverses the classical notion that for metaphor to exist, there must be a non-metaphorical usage for comparison. And regarding Being, the problem that arose at the conceptual level – does Being have being or not? – reappears at the verbal level – does the word 'Being' have a literal meaning when there is no figurative meaning to compare it to? This question appears unanswerable, which is precisely Derrida's point: the constant, vigilant repositing of this question in different forms constitutes what Derrida calls 'deconstruction'. For Derrida, deconstruction is not a manifestation of 'suspicion', as Ricoeur claims it is, but an affirmation of the ability of metaphysics to incorporate its own negation within itself.

HEIDEGGER, LANGUAGE AND DECONSTRUCTION

Despite Derrida's claimed affinity with some of Ricoeur's ideas, this detour through Derrida's response to Ricoeur's criticism of him is designed to show the differences between the two thinkers. In literary criticism, theology and biblical hermeneutics, critics and theologians have been drawn to Ricoeur as a less radical alternative to Derrida. Their differences come down to different ways of conceiving language and different ways of responding to Heidegger. Heidegger (1971: 146 and 215) famously claimed that 'Man acts as though *he* were the shaper and master of language, while in fact *language* remains the master of man.' Both Derrida and Ricoeur build their philosophies on this premise, but in different ways. In his introduction to a collection of Ricoeur essays aimed specifically at literature students (*A Ricoeur Reader:*

Reflection and Imagination, 1991), Mario J. Valdés (1991: 25) notes that 'Derrida and Ricoeur share in . . . Heidegger's conception of human existence that rules out the possibility of an errorless reliable origin'. Timothy Clark, meanwhile, in his Routledge Critical Thinkers *Martin Heidegger* (2002: 146), points out that Ricoeur's answer to his own question posited in the essay 'The Hermeneutical Function of Distanciation', 'What remains to be interpreted?', is a Heideggerian one: 'What must be interpreted in a text is a *proposed world* which I could inhabit and wherein I could project my ownmost possibilities' (Ricoeur 1991a: 86).

However, notwithstanding these common affinities and their shared appreciation of Heidegger, there are marked differences between the philosophies of Derrida and Ricoeur. We have seen one difference in our discussion of metaphor. Another is that for Ricoeur, appropriation is a counterpart to distanciation: it is what the distanciating effect of writing, and of the consequent disappearance of the author from determining the meaning of a text, allows the reader to do. Meanwhile, in the words of Clark (2002: 47), 'Heidegger is fascinated by that element of the work that resists appropriation, that cannot be stabilised by interpretation, or made compatible with the work of worldly meaning', and Derrida shares this fascination. Consequent upon this difference between the two thinkers is a difference in conceiving where the 'dialectic' lies. For Ricoeur, the dialectic is between the text and the reader: when a reader engages in dialectical relation with a text, the result 'is not a question of imposing upon the text our finite capacity for understanding, but of exposing ourselves to the text and receiving from it an enlarged self' (Ricoeur 1991a: 88). Hence, the dialectic increases understanding. For Derrida, the dialectic is played out within the text itself, between its capacity for meaning and the dependence of that capacity on the possibility of the text's meaning something else. Hence, the dialectic only increases understanding by simultaneously diminishing it, through our being dazzled by the myriad display of other possible interpretations. Moreover, the two terms of this dialectic (meaning and its possible other) do not resolve themselves into one, but are maintained in interminable suspense. The laying bare of that suspense constitutes the critical activity that is deconstruction.

Ricoeur appeals to those who would cling to some sort of authority for referential meaning in the face of the alleged assault upon it (upon the authority, if not upon the referential meaning) by Derridean decon-struction. For Ricoeur (1991a: 85), although in literature 'language seems to glorify itself at the expense of the referential function of ordi-nary discourse', nevertheless 'there is no discourse so fictional that it does not connect up with reality'. And not only does Ricoeur rescue ref-erential meaning for appropriation by understanding, he also goes some way towards rescuing the author from his own Barthesian assault. It would be wrong, he says, simply to dismiss authorial intention as a cri-terion for the interpretation of a work, and put in its place 'the fallacy of the absolute text: the fallacy of hypostatising the text as an authorless entity' (Ricoeur 1976: 30). Rather, the relationship between meaning in the sense of 'what the author intended' and meaning in the sense of 'what the text says' must also be conceived of dialectically: 'the autho-rial meaning is the dialectical counterpart of the verbal meaning, and they have to be construed in terms of each other' (Ricoeur 1976: 30).

READING THE BIBLE AS LITERATURE

It is in this respect that Ricoeur has become important to theology, and especially to the interpretation of religious texts, since at some level they are held to be the word of God. Holy scriptures embody the Ricoeur version of the dialectic of reading. That they were written by anonymous scribes points up the distinction between the mere writer or scriptor, and the 'author' whose intentions are embodied in the text. It is the task of the reader to engage dialectically with these intentions by reappropriating them through a work of reading – interpreting – which the distanciating effect of their having been written makes possible. As Ricoeur (1991a: 99) writes in his essay 'Philosophical and Biblical Hermeneutics' (1975),

> Biblical faith cannot be separated from the movement of interpretation that raises it to the level of language. The 'ultimate care' would remain *mute* if it did not receive the power of speech from an endlessly renewed interpretation of the signs and symbols that have, so to speak, educated and formed this care throughout the centuries.

In other words, it is the fact of their having been written that causes the Scriptures to invite themselves to be interpreted. When the text to be read is the Bible, the 'wager' of the hermeneutic circle – that my hypothesised reading will turn out to be the true one – is transformed into faith as such.

In this spirit the theologian James Fodor, in his book *Christian Hermeneutics* (1995), draws on Ricoeur to address the question of reference in theological statements: to what are the propositions of theology referring, and in what sense are they true? According to Fodor, interpreting theological statements involves a process of 'refiguration', a term taken from Ricoeur's analysis of narrative. Fodor agrees with Ricoeur in the claim that life as such is understood as a narrative and that therefore we can bring a narrative pre-understanding to texts, which are then 'completed' by the reader in the process of reading, but he then extends Ricoeur's theory to language in general, finding in all of our linguistic practices a potential for this refiguring ability. It is by utilising this ability that the referential truth of theological statements comes to be revealed, which constitutes a defence of such truth-claims on the part of theology in the face of criticism that they are relative, subjective or nominalist (i.e. merely words referring to other words).

For Ricoeur, 'appropriation' of the meaning of a text by a reader opens up the referential function of the text to a new level, that of how we live in the world: poetry and fiction refer to truths, and the truths to which they refer are the truths of how it is to be in the world. Fodor extends this notion of the work of appropriation creating the referential truth of literature to Scripture, where the reference to truth that the reader's appropriation of Scripture facilitates is knowledge of God. 'Apprehended as a whole', says Fodor (1995: 252), 'the Bible forms one large living intertext where its constitutive heterogeneous elements are allowed to work on one another, simultaneously displacing their respective meanings but also mutually drawing upon their overall dynamism'. The juxtaposition of genres within the Bible is not a threat to its capacity to tell truth, but is, rather, the means by which 'a veritable augmentation of meaning occurs' (Fodor 1995: 252).

Meanwhile Kevin J. Vanhoozer, in his *Biblical Narrative in the Philosophy of Paul Ricoeur* (1990), also provides an explication of Ricoeur's hermeneutics, with particular reference to his theory of narrative, in order to explore how specifically Biblical narrative functions, again in order to defend the truth of that narrative. What Fodor and Vanhoozer both realise is that Ricoeur's hermeneutics allows the claim that the Bible refers to truths in a meaningful way, not so much despite, but *because of*, the Bible being not 'literally' true at the level of specific 'facts' (such as in its assertion, say, that the world was created in six days).

Another contemporary theologian, Craig Bartholomew, is particularly impressed by Ricoeur's hermeneutics of revelation, returning to *The Symbolism of Evil*'s insistence on the symbols of revelation, rather than the propositions of reason, as the key to faith and the understanding of faith (Bartholomew 1998: 24). However, he shares with Nicholas Wolterstorff a reading of Ricoeur which places him in closer alignment with Derrida, to whom both Bartholomew and Wolterstorff are opposed, on the grounds that Derrida's philosophy is incompatible with what Wolterstorff (1995: 162) calls 'authorial-discourse interpretation'. Wolterstorff's (1995: 1) project is not only to 'reflect philosophically on the claim that God speaks', but also to defend that claim. Hence he is keen to defend *speech* as opposed to *writing* as a source of authority, and the *speaker* (in this case, God) as a source of meaning in language. Consequently, and in contradistinction to Bartholomew, Wolterstorff (1995: 58–9) is unimpressed by Ricoeur's privileging of revelation: 'By the time [Ricoeur] has finished, divine speech has disappeared from view and only revelation of the manifestation sort is left.' This leads to the further charge that Ricoeur 'does not ask how the concept of revelation functions in the religious lives of Jews and Christians; he does not even ask how it functions in the sacred writings of Jews and Christians' (Wolterstorff 1995: 59). Wolterstorff's (1995: 62) argument is that while Ricoeur is right to 'resist assimilating divine revelation to divine speech', it is equally erroneous 'to assimilate divine speech to divine revelation'. He goes on:

> A striking feature of Ricoeur's discussion is his complete neglect of the fact that attributions of speech to God pervade all the discourse-genres of the Bible: narrative, prescriptive, hymnic, even wisdom. In all of them, speech is attributed to God.
>
> (Wolterstorff 1995: 62)

As an alternative to Ricoeur's theory, Wolterstorff proposes a model of *discourse* appropriating other discourse, as opposed to the *reader* appropriating discourse. Scripture, for Wolterstorff, is already an example of appropriation: of the speech of God by the writings of the prophets who set them down. Hence the words of Scripture do not so much invite interpretation, but manifest an already-interpreted truth. And consequently, the words of Scripture do not work like fiction: another possible world is not opened up to the reader, but rather, the real world of God's truth is revealed, not as manifestation, but as language.

In similar vein, Anthony C. Thiselton, in his book *New Horizons in Hermeneutics* (1992), sees Scripture not as a collection of texts, as Ricoeur does, but rather as an 'address' to an addressee who is conceived not as a reader, but as a listener, denying Ricoeur's claim that the fact of the Bible's having been written down irrevocably alters the way in which it is, or should be, received.

A theologian much more sympathetic to Ricoeur is Douglas Burton-Christie in his *The Word in the Desert* (1993). Burton-Christie's book is an interpretation of *The Sayings of the Desert Fathers*, the desert fathers being 'a motley band of colourful characters' (Burton-Christie 1993: vii) who lived a hermit-like existence in fourth-century Egypt. Given that theirs was primarily an oral culture, it is perhaps surprising that Burton-Christie should adopt Ricoeur's written-text-based model of discourse. But for Burton-Christie, Ricoeur's 'dialectic of event and meaning' is a powerful tool for explaining how the sayings of God and the desert elders came to endure over time. The *saying* of the sayings is an event, something that has the capacity to change people's lives (to re-evaluate the shallowness of their previous lives and go and live in the desert, for example). The *meaning* of the sayings, meanwhile, is a continuing process which endures, nourished as it is by the ongoing contemplation of the sayings which constitutes a large part of desert life. So, the speech-event prompts a *new* understanding of life, but the meaning contributes to *deeper* understanding of life. Moreover, Burton-Christie is impressed by Ricoeur's insistence on the ability of a text to project a world. This is once again dependent on the ability of the sayings to *refer*, 'the movement in which language transcends itself and expresses a world' (Burton-Christie 1993: 19). The sayings of God and the desert elders really did change the lives, or the ways-of-being-in-the-world, of those who heard them, in the very real sense that they forsook their worldly possessions and went off to live in the desert – a movement from text to action, in Ricoeur's terms. Or, as Burton-Christie (1993: 20) elucidates:

> Because there was so much emphasis in the desert on practice, on living with integrity, the monks interpreted Scripture primarily by putting it into practice.

In the desert, Scripture's surplus of meaning endured not in the form of commentaries or homilies but in acts or gestures, in lives of holiness transformed by dialogue with Scripture. The sacred texts continued to mean more not only to those who read or encountered the texts but also to those encountering the holy ones who had come to embody the texts. The holy person became a new text and a new object of interpretation.

It is a similar destiny that awaits Paul Ricoeur himself in the years to come.

FURTHER READING

WORKS BY PAUL RICOEUR

Ricoeur, Paul (1950) *Philosophie de la volonté. I. Le volontaire et l'involontaire*, Paris: Aubier. (English version 1966, *Freedom and Nature: The Voluntary and the Involuntary*, trans. E. V. Kohák, Evanston: Northwestern University Press.)

The first part of the projected three-part *Philosophy of the Will*. Heavily influenced by Edmund Husserl, but also the first of Ricoeur's works to criticise Husserl, especially in terms of the place of the 'passions' in Husserl's thought. Contains Ricoeur's first systematic critique of the Cartesian *cogito*, asserting a Christian 'materialism' that denies the duality of mind and body, and instead demonstrates that thinking can itself only be thought, or perceived, through the existential given, or 'mystery', of having a body.

—— (1955; 2nd edn 1964) *Histoire et vérité*, Paris: Seuil. (English version 1965, *History and Truth*, trans. Charles A. Kebley, Evanston: Northwestern University Press.)

A collection of early essays on the meaning of history, of what constitutes history, and on the relationship between history and religion. The second edition, which is the source for the English translation, also contains four essays on political philosophy, including the important 'State and Violence' and 'The Political Paradox', and concludes with 'Negativity and Primary Affirmation', a veiled attack on Sartre's atheism.

—— (1960) *Philosophie de la volonté. Finitude et Culpabilité. I. L'homme faillible*, Paris: Aubier. (English version 1965, *Fallible Man*, trans. Charles A. Kelbley, Chicago: Regnery.)

The first half of the second part of *Philosophy of the Will*. An investigation into why man is fallible, or prone to succumbing to moral fault. Investigates imagination, character and feeling as points of 'disproportion' between the involuntary and the voluntary, points which are necessary to man's constitution, but at which he is most likely to err.

—— (1960) *Philosophie de la volonté. Finitude et Culpabilité. II. La symbolique du mal*, Paris: Aubier. (English version 1967, *The Symbolism of Evil*, trans. Emerson Buchanan, Boston: Beacon.)

The second half of the second part of *Philosophy of the Will* (the third part was never written), itself divided into two parts. The first part analyses confession, defilement, sin and guilt in broadly phenomenological terms, demonstrating how they represent a movement from the action of an exterior agent, to a transgression on the part of the subject, to that transgression's interiorisation. The second part analyses how myths are symbolic of this progression of thought. The conclusion, 'The Symbol Gives Rise to Thought', is one of Ricoeur's most important texts, being a clear, succinct (and his earliest) exposition of his theory of hermeneutics.

—— (1965) *De l'interprétation. Essai sur Freud*, Paris: Seuil. (English version 1970, *Freud and Philosophy: An Essay on Interpretation*, trans. Denis Savage, New Haven and London: Yale University Press.)

Ricoeur's first full-length book to be fully informed by his theory of hermeneutics. Attempts to reconcile Freudian psychoanalysis with phenomenology, by seeing the former as primarily a hermeneutic practice. Divided into a 'Problematic', which reprises the descriptions of hermeneutics to be found at the end of *The Symbolism of Evil*, but with specific relevance to Freud, an 'Analytic', or exposition of Freud's texts, and a 'Dialectic', which posits the value of symbols as revelations of truth against Freud's view that they intend to deceive, with specific reference to art and religion.

—— (1969) *Le conflit des interprétations. Essais d'herméneutique*, Paris: Seuil. (English version 1974, *The Conflict of Interpretations: Essays in Hermeneutics*, ed. Don Ihde, Evanston: Northwestern University Press.)

Essays written throughout the 1960s on the relationship between hermeneutics and other disciplines or fields of discourse. The section on 'Hermeneutics and Psychoanalysis' supplements the 'Analytic' section of *Freud and Philosophy*, and the section 'The Symbolism of Evil Interpreted' refines the position set out at the end of *The Symbolism of Evil*. Also includes the important essay 'The Problem of Double Meaning as Hermeneutic Problem and as Semantic Problem', which marks the development of hermeneutics away from mere symbol interpretation to the interpretation of discourse as a whole.

—— (1975) *La métaphore vive*, Paris: Seuil. (English version 1977, *The Rule of Metaphor: Multi-Disciplinary Studies of the Creation of Meaning in Language*, trans. Robert Czerny with Kathleen McLaughlin and John Costello, Toronto and Buffalo: University of Toronto Press.)

A comprehensive study of metaphor, from its operations at the level of the word, the sentence, and discourse, to its operation within the discipline of philosophy as a whole.

—— (1976) *Interpretation Theory: Discourse and the Surplus of Meaning*, Fort Worth: Texas Christian University Press.

A slim volume, but one of Ricoeur's most influential in literary theory and biblical hermeneutics in the English-speaking world. Fleshes out the themes found in some of the essays collected in *From Text to Action* (see below), such as the distinctions between language and discourse, and between speech and writing. Especially important for developing the notions of distanciation, the 'semantic autonomy' of the text, and interpretation as an 'appropriation' of meaning by the reader. Unpublished in French.

—— (1981) *Hermeneutics and the Human Sciences: Essays on Language, Action and Interpretation*, trans. and ed. John B. Thompson, Cambridge: Cambridge University Press. Contains eleven essays (six of which are reproduced in *From Text to Action*; see below), including 'The Narrative Function' (1979), Ricoeur's first work on narrative, and in some ways a summary of much of that which is to follow.

—— (1983) *Temps et récit. Tome I*, Paris: Seuil. (English version 1984, *Time and Narrative, Volume 1*, trans. Kathleen McLaughlin and David Pellauer, Chicago and London: University of Chicago Press.)

Contains Part I, 'The Circle of Narrative and Temporality', and Part II, 'History and Narrative'. Part I establishes the distinctions of 'threefold mimesis' (prefiguration, configuration and refiguration), and restates the 'hermeneutic circle' as a virtuous circle no longer merely at the level of understanding individual sentences or self-contained discourses, but at an extended textual level: all of life can be read as a narrative text, and vice versa. Part II justifies seeing history writing as a form of narrative, and refines the concept of 'historical truth' first mooted in *Freud and Philosophy*.

—— (1984) *Temps et récit. Tome II. La configuration dans le récit de fiction*, Paris: Seuil. (English version, 1985, *Time and Narrative, Volume 2*, trans. Kathleen McLaughlin and David Pellauer, Chicago and London: University of Chicago Press.)

Contains Part III, 'The Configuration of Time in Fictional Narrative', which reads three novels – Virginia Woolf's *Mrs Dalloway*, Thomas Mann's *Magic Mountain* and Marcel Proust's *Remembrance of Things Past* – as exemplary works about time itself. Ricoeur's most sustained foray into literary criticism.

—— (1985) *Temps et récit. Tome III. Le temps raconté*, Paris: Seuil. (English version 1985, *Time and Narrative, Volume 3*, trans. Kathleen Blamey and David Pellauer, Chicago and London: University of Chicago Press.)

Contains Part IV, 'Narrated Time'. Concludes that narrated time is the time of life, and conceives an essential unity between historical narrative, which is seen as a duty of the remembrance of the dead, and fictional narrative, which is seen as an expression of man's capacity to project himself into the point of view of other people, and is hence an opening into ethics. Consequently, a 'good story' must be morally good to be aesthetically satisfying.

—— (1986) *Du texte à l'action. Essais d'herméneutique*, Paris, Seuil. (English version 1991, *From Text to Action: Essays in Hermeneutics, II*, trans. Kathleen Blamey and John B. Thompson, Evanston: Northwestern University Press.)

The sequel to *The Conflict of Interpretations*, collecting essays written in the 1970s and early 1980s. They are principally further explanations of the term 'hermeneutics', but also attempting to extend hermeneutics beyond a philosophy of reading into a 'philosophy of action'.

—— (1990) *Soi-même comme un autre*, Paris: Seuil. (English version 1992, *Oneself as Another*, trans. Kathleen Blamey, Chicago and London: University of Chicago Press.)

Continues the ideas developed in *Time and Narrative*, to posit the concept of 'narrative identity': that we gain our identity from the narratives we know, and that such narratives form our moral nourishment. Ricoeur's most sustained work of ethics, containing important material on the promise as guarantor of character, and the intersubjective, reciprocal nature of the ethical transaction involved in keeping one's word to another.

—— (1991) *A Ricoeur Reader: Reflection and Imagination*, ed. Mario J. Valdés, Hemel Hempstead: Harvester Wheatsheaf.

Ricoeur writings collected explicitly with the literary reader in mind. Contains various essays, reviews and interviews from 1970 to 1986, and is useful in showing Ricoeur in debate with some of his contemporaries, such as Gadamer. Valdés' Introduction discusses Ricoeur's theory of text interpretation with particular reference to literature, but is unhelpful in its use of the ill-defined catch-all term 'post-structuralist' to define Ricoeur's hermeneutics.

—— (1995) *Le Juste*, Paris: Ésprit. (English version 2000, *The Just*, trans. David Pellauer, Chicago and London: University of Chicago Press.)

Contains ten self-contained studies on legal theory and politics, which together form a consistent statement of Ricoeur's theory of justice. Of particular interest are the essays 'Is a Purely Procedural Theory of Justice Possible?', which reveals Ricoeur's indebtedness to John Rawls, and 'The Act of Judging', which discusses the role of the third party in progressing from vengeance to justice.

—— (1995) *La Critique et la conviction*, Paris: Calmann-Lévy. (English version 1998, *Critique and Conviction: Conversations with François Azouvi and Marc de Launay*, trans. Kathleen Blamey, Cambridge: Polity.)

Contains eight interviews in which Ricoeur discusses the entire span of his intellectual life, and most areas of his work. Quite personal in tone, they elucidate Ricoeur's ideas on religion, psychoanalysis, aesthetics and politics, and the interview 'Duty of Memory, Duty of Justice' is an invaluable complement to *The Just*. The style is highly accessible, and the book is an excellent place at which to begin reading Ricoeur himself.

—— (1995) *Figuring the Sacred: Religion, Narrative, and Imagination*, trans. David Pellauer, ed. Mark I. Wallace, Minneapolis: Fortress.

An anthology of Ricoeur's essays on religion written in the 1970s and 1980s. Includes 'Ethical and Theological Considerations on the Golden Rule', which complements *The Just*.

WORKS ON PAUL RICOEUR

Clark, S. H. (1990) *Paul Ricoeur*, London and New York: Routledge.

Quite an advanced introduction which presupposes prior knowledge of some of the terms and concepts discussed; critical evaluation is intertwined with the exposition, especially in comparing Ricoeur favourably with his French contemporaries such as Lacan and Derrida. Published in 1990, and so no discussion of *Oneself as Another*, *The Just*, or the later political essays.

Evans, Jeanne (1995) *Paul Ricoeur's Hermeneutics of the Imagination*, New York: Lang.

A somewhat slight volume, largely expository, but useful in tracing the development of Ricoeur's version of hermeneutics within a religious context.

Hahn, Lewis Edwin (ed.) (1995) *The Philosophy of Paul Ricoeur*, Chicago and La Salle: Open Court.

As well as a number of essays on Ricoeur by leading critics, contains Ricoeur's 'Intellectual Autobiography', which makes a good second route into Ricoeur after *Critique and Conviction*. Also contains a comprehensive bibliography of Ricoeur (including primary and secondary texts, and all translations), 1935–95.

Ihde, Don (1971) *Hermeneutic Phenomenology: The Philosophy of Paul Ricoeur*, Evanston: Northwestern University Press.

Despite its date, remains a good critical account of the philosophical (especially phenomenological) background to Ricoeur's hermeneutics, finding a 'latent hermeneutics' in Ricoeur's work prior to *The Symbolism of Evil*. The prose can be a little dense in places.

Kearney, Richard (ed.) (1996) *Paul Ricoeur: The Hermeneutics of Action*, London: Sage.

Contains three important essays on politics and justice by Ricoeur, 'Reflections on a New Ethos for Europe' (1992), 'Fragility and Responsibility' (1992) and 'Love and Justice' (1991), together with essays by Ricoeur scholars on his work in history, ethics, politics etc., as well as reviews of Ricoeur's lectures.

Reagan, Charles E. (1996) *Paul Ricoeur: His Life and Work*, Chicago and London: University of Chicago Press.

Contains a biographical essay, a memoir, a philosophical essay and four interviews with Ricoeur. The biographical essay proves Ricoeur's own thesis, that one's life is a 'work' in the textual sense, to be true of Ricoeur himself, and is moreover a truly riveting read. The philosophical essay is on 'personal identity', and is a good introduction to Ricoeur's views on character, stretching from *The Symbolism of Evil* to *Oneself as Another*.

Wood, David (ed.) (1991) *On Paul Ricoeur: Narrative and Interpretation*, London: Routledge.

As the title implies, the essays concentrate on Ricoeur's *Time and Narrative* and associated texts, but they are all of outstanding quality, and include works by such leading Ricoeur commentators as Richard Kearney, Jonathan Rée and Don Ihde, along with two essays by Ricoeur and a discussion with him. One of the Ricoeur essays, 'Life in Quest of Narrative', constitutes his most explicit argument that there is a 'prenarrative quality of human experience' (Ricoeur 1991c: 29), and that 'a given chain of episodes in our own life [is] something like stories that have not yet been told' (Ricoeur 1991c: 30).

VIDEO

Rée Jonathan (1992) *Talking Liberties*, London: Channel 4 Television/ Praxis Films.

In a forty-minute interview with Jonathan Rée, Ricoeur discusses all of the major areas of his philosophy and intellectual life. A succinct and clear summary of his work. A transcript is also available (Rée, Jonathan (1992) *Talking Liberties*, London: Channel 4 Television).

WEBSITE

http://www.balzan.it/english/pb1999/index.htm.

In 1999 Ricoeur won the Balzan Prize (a kind of Swiss equivalent to the Nobel Prize) for contributions to philosophy. The Balzan website features a profile of Ricoeur, and a synopsis of his work.

WORKS CITED

Aristotle (1991) [*c.* 337 BC] *The Art of Rhetoric*, trans. Hugh Lawson-Tancred, Harmondsworth: Penguin.

—— (1996) [*c.* 337 BC] *Poetics*, trans. Malcolm Heath, Harmondsworth: Penguin.

St Augustine (1991) [*c.* 397] *Confessions*, trans. Edward Bouverie Pusey, New York: Quality Paperback Book Club.

Barthes, Roland (1977) [1966] 'The Death of the Author', in *Image, Music, Text*, ed. and trans. Stephen Heath, London: Fontana.

Bartholomew, Craig G. (1998) *Reading Ecclesiastes: Old Testament Exegesis and Hermeneutical Theory*, Rome: Pontifical Biblical Institute.

Beardsley, Monroe C. (1958) *Aesthetics*, New York: Harcourt, Brace & World.

—— (1962) 'The Metaphorical Twist', *Philosophy and Phenomenological Research* 22: 293–307.

Black, Max (1962) *Models and Metaphors: Studies in Language and Philosophy*, Ithaca: Cornell University Press.

Burton-Christie, Douglas (1993) *The Word in the Desert: Scripture and the Quest for Holiness in Early Christian Monasticism*, New York and Oxford: Oxford University Press.

Clark, S. H. (1990) *Paul Ricoeur*, London and New York: Routledge.

Clark, Timothy (2002) *Martin Heidegger*, London and New York: Routledge.

Derrida, Jacques (1982) [1971] 'White Mythology', in *Margins of Philosophy*, trans. Alan Bass, Brighton: Harvester.

—— (1998) [1978] 'The *Retrait* of Metaphor', trans. F. Gasdner, in Julian Wolfreys (ed.), *The Derrida Reader: Writing Performances*, Edinburgh: Edinburgh University Press.

Dostoevesky, Fyodor (1972) [1864] *Notes from the Underground*, trans. Jessie Coulson, Harmondsworth: Penguin.

Evans, Jean (1995) *Paul Ricoeur's Hermeneutics of the Imagination*, New York: Lang.

Fielding, Henry (1992) [1749] *The History of Tom Jones, A Foundling*, Ware: Wordsworth.

Fodor, James (1995) *Christian Hermeneutics: Paul Ricoeur and the Refiguring of Theology*, Oxford: Clarendon.

Freud, Sigmund (1973) [1932] *New Introductory Lectures on Psychoanalysis*, trans. James Strachey, ed. James Strachey and Angela Richards, Harmondsworth: Penguin.

—— (1976) [1899] *The Interpretation of Dreams*, trans. James Strachey, ed. James Strachey, Alan Tyson and Angela Richards, Harmondsworth: Penguin.

Gadamer, Hans-Georg (1989) [1960] *Truth and Method*, trans. Joel Weinsheimer and Donald G. Marshall, London: Sheed & Ward, 2nd edn.

Hahn, Lewis Edwin (ed.) (1995) *The Philosophy of Paul Ricoeur*, Chicago and La Salle: Open Court.

Heidegger, Martin (1962) [1927] *Being and Time*, trans. John Macquarrie and Edward Robinson, Oxford: Blackwell.

—— (1971) *Poetry, Language, Thought*, trans. Albert Hofstadter, New York: Harper.

Ihde, Don (1971) *Hermeneutic Phenomenology: The Philosophy of Paul Ricoeur*, Evanston: Northwestern University Press.

Jakobson, Roman (1971) *Selected Writings II: Word and Language*, The Hague and Paris: Mouton.

Kearney, Richard (ed.) (1996) *Paul Ricoeur: The Hermeneutics of Action*, London: Sage.

Kermode, Frank (1966) *The Sense of an Ending: Studies in the Theory of Fiction*, New York and Oxford: Oxford University Press.

King, Martin Luther, Jr (1963) 'I Have a Dream', http://web66.coled.umn.edu/new/MLK/MLK.html.

Mink, Louis O. (1970) 'History and Fiction as Modes of Comprehension', *New Literary History* 1, 541–58.

Nietzsche, Friedrich (1979) [1873] 'On Truth and Lies in a Non-Moral Sense', in *Philosophy and Truth: Selections from Nietzsche's Notebooks of the Early 1870's*, trans. and ed. Daniel Breazeale, Brighton: Harvester.

Rawls, John (1972) [1971] *A Theory of Justice*, Oxford: Clarendon.

Reagan, Charles E. (1996) *Paul Ricoeur: His Life and His Work*, Chicago and London: University of Chicago Press.

Rée, Jonathan (1992a) *Talking Liberties*, London: Channel 4 Television.

—— (1992b) *Talking Liberties* [video], London: Channel 4 Television/Praxis Films.

Richards, I. A. (1936) *The Philosophy of Rhetoric*, Oxford: Oxford University Press.

Ricoeur, Paul (1965a) [1960] *Fallible Man*, trans. Charles A. Kelbley, Chicago: Regnery.

—— (1965b) [1955; 2nd edn 1964] *History and Truth*, trans. Charles A. Kelbley, Evanston: Northwestern University Press.

—— (1966) [1950] *Freedom and Nature: The Voluntary and the Involuntary*, trans. E. V. Kohák, Evanston: Northwestern University Press.

—— (1967) [1960] *The Symbolism of Evil*, trans. Emerson Buchanan, Boston: Beacon.

—— (1970) [1965] *Freud and Philosophy: An Essay on Interpretation*, trans. Denis Savage, New Haven and London: Yale University Press.

—— (1974) [1969] *The Conflict of Interpretations: Essays in Hermeneutics*, ed. Don Ihde, Evanston: Northwestern University Press.

—— (1976) *Interpretation Theory: Discourse and the Surplus of Meaning*, Fort Worth: Texas Christian University Press.

—— (1977) [1975] *The Rule of Metaphor: Multi-Disciplinary Studies of the Creation of Meaning in Language*, trans. Robert Czerny with Kathleen McLaughlin and John Costello, Toronto and Buffalo: University of Toronto Press.

—— (1981) *Hermeneutics and the Human Sciences: Essays on Language, Action and Interpretation*, trans. and ed. John B. Thompson, Cambridge: Cambridge University Press.

—— (1984) [1983] *Time and Narrative, Volume 1*, trans. Kathleen McLaughlin and David Pellauer, Chicago and London: University of Chicago Press.

—— (1985) [1984] *Time and Narrative, Volume 2*, trans. Kathleen McLaughlin and David Pellauer, Chicago and London: University of Chicago Press.

—— (1988) [1985] *Time and Narrative, Volume 3*, trans. Kathleen Blamey and David Pellauer, Chicago and London: University of Chicago Press.

—— (1991a) [1986] *From Text to Action: Essays in Hermeneutics, II*, trans. Kathleen Blamey and John B. Thompson, London: Athlone.

—— (1991b) *A Ricoeur Reader: Reflection and Imagination*, ed. Mario J. Valdés, Hemel Hempstead: Harvester Wheatsheaf.

—— (1991c) 'Life in Quest of Narrative', in David Wood (ed.) *On Paul Ricoeur: Narrative and Interpretation*, London and New York: Routledge.

—— (1992) [1990] *Oneself as Another*, trans. Kathleen Blamey, Chicago and London: University of Chicago Press.

—— (1995a) 'Intellectual Autobiography', trans. Kathleen Blamey, in Lewis Edwin Hahn (ed.) *The Philosophy of Paul Ricoeur*, Chicago and La Salle: Open Court.

—— (1995b) *Figuring the Sacred: Religion, Narrative, and Imagination*, trans. David Pellauer, ed. Mark I. Wallace, Minneapolis: Fortress.

—— (1996a) 'Love and Justice', trans. David Pellauer, in Richard Kearney (ed.) *Paul Ricoeur: The Hermeneutics of Action*, London: Sage.

—— (1996b) 'Fragility and Responsibility', trans. Elisabeth Iwanowski, in Richard Kearney (ed.) *Paul Ricoeur: The Hermeneutics of Action*, London: Sage.

—— (1998) [1995] *Critique and Conviction: Conversations with François Azouvi and Marc de Launay*, trans. Kathleen Blamey, Cambridge: Polity.

—— (2000) [1995] *The Just*, trans. David Pellauer, Chicago and London: University of Chicago Press.

—— (forthcoming) [1989] 'Power and Violence', trans. Lisa Jones, *Theory, Culture & Society*.

Sophocles (1954) [*c*. 426 BC] *Oedipus the King*, trans. David Grene, in David Grene and Richard Latimore (eds), *Sophocles I*, Chicago and London: University of Chicago Press.

Taylor, Charles (1985) *Human Agency and Language: Philosophical Papers 1*, Cambridge: Cambridge University Press.

Thiselton, Anthony C. (1992) *New Horizons in Hermeneutics*, Grand Rapids: Zondervan.

Valdés, Mario J. (ed.) (1991) 'Introduction: Paul Ricoeur's Post-Structuralist Hermeneutics', in Paul Ricoeur, *A Ricoeur Reader: Reflection and Imagination*, Hemel Hempstead: Harvester Wheatsheaf.

Vanhoozer, Kevin J. (1990) *Biblical Narrative in the Philosophy of Paul Ricoeur: A Study in Hermeneutics*, Cambridge: Cambridge University Press.

Wolterstorff, Nicholas (1995) *Divine Discourse: Philosophical Reflections on the Claim that God Speaks*, Cambridge: Cambridge University Press.

Wood, David (ed.) (1991) *On Paul Ricoeur: Narrative and Interpretation*, London and New York: Routledge.

INDEX

Note: References in **bold type** identify a glossary box.